A LIFE WITH UFOs

A LIFE WITH UFOs

AN INCREDIBLE TRUE STORY

Ray Groschen

Ray Groschen

Self-Published

CONTENTS

DEDICATION viii
INTRODUCTION TO THE GIFT ix

1 | UFO over Pipe Lake 1

2 | 2 UFOs Over the Mississippi 18

3 | UFO Above 7-Eleven 37

4 | UFO over Grand Avenue 58

5 | 27 White UFO Orbs 70

6 | 16 UFOs Above House 84

7 | UFO Flies Into a Wormhole 96

8 | Black Triangular UFO in My Backyard 112

9 | These are not Satellites or The Bewitching Hours 127

10 | The Alien Agenda 149

CONTENTS

ABOUT THE AUTHOR 175
ACKNOWLEDGMENTS 179

A Life with UFOs: An Incredible True Story © 2020
All RIGHTS RESERVED
No part of this publication may be reproduced, distributed, or transmitted in any form or by any means, including photocopying, recording, or other electronic or mechanical methods, without the prior written permission of the publisher, except in the case of brief quotations embodied in critical reviews and certain other noncommercial uses permitted by copyright law. For permission requests, write to the publisher at the address below.

FOR INFORMATION CONTACT: info@raygroschen.com
Library of Congress Control Number: 2019913524

This book is dedicated to my wife and best friend Sharon. And to my children Tony and Steve and grandchildren Blake and Kenna.

INTRODUCTION TO THE GIFT

This is a true story about a remarkable journey through my adult life and the gift somehow given to me from the universe at large. I am inextricably bound to UFOs and UFOs to me. Like the moon is linked to the earth and the earth to the moon. This precious gift represents an ability to intuit when a UFO is nearby and taking myself to that place at the right time. The bestowal has been my destiny since 1975 when I and others with me first witnessed a UFO.

I could have received the gift from the beings in those UFOs. Because once I'm at that place where they are, I get this eerie feeling like someone is staring at me. I'm sure you think that hey, this is nothing unusual; we all have those same feelings. Like when someone is staring at you from another car when driving next to them down a road. I understand, but with me, it is invariably a UFO.

No matter what I'm doing or where the universe takes me, sooner or later, a UFO or a group of UFOs show up. Usually, they see me before I see them. Still, I always witness an excellent show.

This gift could be construed as a consecrated gift since so many witnesses have shouted, "Holy Crap or Oh My God, it's a UFO!" And I have screamed OH MY GOD more than I can count!

Since this has happened to me for most of my adult life, I shout the same thing with the same enthusiasm, but I can also look at what is happening more scientifically. That's because I'm not scared anymore when I witness a UFO. I was terrified seeing my first one, but since none of the UFOs I've seen haven't made any threatening moves toward me, I can relax and take in the show and gather data on the experience.

I have yet to figure out how or why the universe or the beings on those UFOs bestowed me with this glorious honor, but indeed it was unexpected. Even seemed undeserving in the breadth of its totality. Over most of my adult life, I've had 20 separate UFO sightings culminating in identifying a total of 74 ships of eight different designs. And if that wasn't enough, I witnessed a UFO fly into a wormhole!

I now know that the places I have lived in or have visited at certain times have been to experience incredible sightings of UFOs. I've come to realize that there is more to my life than just me deciding on where to live. I have always wondered why I've had a strong feeling about a particular place. I seem to disregard friends and family advice to the contrary. Really? You're going to move where? Phoenix, Arizona? Are you sure you want to move there? I would make excuses like I hated the winters in Minnesota, where I grew up. When, in fact, most things don't bother me much. Instead, I would listen to my intuition, not yet knowing why the universe wanted me to experience those places.

I have had so many UFO sightings that I don't believe it was luck or a coincidence, in the same way as if I'd won the lottery 20 times. No way. There has to be more to it than that. The more logical explanation would be that I had a system.

I have come to understand that this gift is precious and a type of communication. I would not hear things in my head like if it were a telepathic type of communication. It's that I get a feeling, an urge if you will, to do something I didn't want to do. Or to go outside when I don't want to.

The following is an example of how it happens; one night, I woke up at approximately 2:00 am and went outside. I didn't want to go out, but something somewhere was driving me, pulling me to go outside. It was such an urge, such a strange and eerie feeling I had that I couldn't resist. Like being hypnotized with my arms out saying I'm in your power. What can I do for you, master?

Because of my disability, it's nothing unusual for me to wake up from the pain, but it was completely different on this night. If and when I do wake in the night, I routinely take a pair of binoculars with me to look at the stars. After I woke up and went outside, I lay down on my patio chair and started scanning the sky. I put the binoculars up to my eyes and peered overhead. When I looked through the binoculars at that exact moment and location, I saw a swarm of round UFOs flying right over my house. Maybe a few thousand feet up. Why did I look precisely where I did? I could have looked anywhere above or around me, but that's my intuition again. That's the gift working. My intuition is the gift. I trust my instincts above all other things because I've never been disappointed with the results.

I know they can be anywhere and at any time, but for me to wake at that particular time of night and catch these UFOs flying overhead right then? It just cannot always be a coincidence. They must have communicated something to me. To pull me outside and to lay down on my patio chair and look where I did. I just can't be that lucky. I am not buying that. Again, if I was that lucky, then why haven't I won the lottery?

The gift or communication that shows up for me as intuition has brought me to places that have led to superb and spectacular sightings. I could be fishing with my son on the Mississippi River or sitting out on my patio with my wife, and a UFO appears. They must have communicated something to me so I would show up at those places to see them.

INTRODUCTION TO THE GIFT

There have been some rare occasions where I thought luck had been on my side. I used to think it could be luck, but I wasn't quite sure. Now I know it's not luck, but the gift working as it always has been. I was casually peering through my telescope at the stars in the sky when one of those stars just started to move. What are the odds of me looking through my telescope, and a star-like object just happens to move? Was it just pure dumb luck, or was I meant to be looking at that star at that moment? I know one thing is for sure, stars don't move like that, nor do satellites.

All of these sightings will be in the chapter, 'These are Not Satellites.' If you think that all those little points of lights you see in the night sky are stars, well, think again. I call these types of sightings minor.

Minor sightings are star-like objects that I cannot identify other than them being points of light in the night sky. Similar to a satellite going across the sky. They only look like points of light because they are above our atmosphere, making them too far away to discern. Even if I had my telescope fixed on them, I wouldn't be able to see the actual satellite, just the light reflecting off its surface.

I've had many minor sightings of these star-like UFOs stopping, starting, and making U-turns. I've seen a couple of UFOs, again star-like objects that meet up with three others, and away they went—all five going to who knows where.

Whenever I witness an actual UFO craft that is near me, I try my hardest to document the experience because my memory is fading and fading fast. I call these sightings major. The last major sighting was in 2015, but I'm hoping beyond hope I see more UFOs.

What I mean to say about a major sighting is I'm referring to a sighting where there is an actual ship or multiple ships close to me where I can define their characteristics. I have had major and minor UFO sightings from Cumberland, Wisconsin, to St. Paul, Minnesota, and from my home in Phoenix, Arizona.

Was it me who had the feeling to go fishing or out on the patio or look through the telescope at the exact time? Or were they already there and were sending me a message to get a glimpse of them? I think it's all because of the gift and not some government plot.

I'm not big on conspiracy theories, so I try and rationalize things as best I can. I don't believe that the government is involved with everything that's out of the ordinary. I don't think they control our minds with fluoride toothpaste; that Princess Diana was murdered; that the American government knew about the 9/11 attacks in advance and chose to let them happen, and so on. Thinking about that stuff can drive a person insane. And I don't think the government is involved with any of my UFO sightings either.

Although I have wondered with a humorous analogy, maybe I'm the deer in the woods, and whoever is on board those ships is the biologist tracking my patterns. And perhaps they even tagged me because the wife and I have had some peculiar occurrences during the night. Of course, if I were a person who believed in conspiracy theories, I wouldn't think that what has happened to us at night is nothing more than everyday occurrences. To keep my sanity, I just can't go there. I have to believe these things are typical conditions that happen to all of us during the night.

Sharon and I have found scratch marks on both our bodies in the mornings in impossible to reach places. My wife, Sharon, woke up one morning with a small triangular object under the skin near her wrist. It was rigid like a rock, and you could easily make out a triangular object under her skin. I'm not sure just how long she had it there, but one day she woke, and it was gone. Most people would explain these away as everyday occurrences. I'm not saying that I'm not worried, but I do wonder just how these things might have happened.

I have also experienced some other strange occurrences during the night. My snoring used to be an issue that woke me a lot at night, but I've taken care of that with the C-Pap machine.

C-Pap stands for Continuous Positive Airflow Pressure. It's a small machine that sits on my nightstand next to the bed that provides continuous airflow into my throat. It blows air through a long hose with a mask connected to the end, keeping my airway open so that I won't snore. One morning I woke to find the C-Pap mask put on wrong. As if a person woke up one morning to find their pajama top put on backward. There was absolutely no way I could have done this, and that freaked me out a bit. Luckily, that has never happened again.

We have a wonderful little son, Lincoln, who we bought from a shelter maybe five years ago. He is an 18-pound black and grey tabby cat. When we first got him, he was an extremely calm cat, but we noticed some very odd behavior within a short time. Several months after getting him, he became scared. He jumps at the smallest movement or sound. He can't come into a room without sinking low to the ground and twitching at anything on the floor.

I could explain all these away as everyday occurrences, but there's a part of me that wonders if they have come into our home and abducted us. I don't know if I have been or not. I just know that I don't want to find out. I'm happy the way I am. I'm not going to go and get hypnotized to find out that they have been in our home.

Or at least gave us false memories of being abducted. There are government splinter groups that have the technology to fake an abduction. I truly do NOT believe that aliens abduct anyone. I think our government does fake abductions and use this ruse to keep us thinking that aliens are some kind of threat. Aliens are not a threat!

They are a highly evolved civilization that is spiritually higher than we are and are showing themselves so we understand that they are here to help us not hurt us. Trust me when I say that if they were a threat they could have destroyed this planet eons ago.

I am disabled and have been since 2008. I cannot sleep through the night without waking several times because of the pain I'm in. I have Degenerative Disc Disease, which is an age-related condition. What happens is that one or more of the discs between the vertebrae of the spinal column deteriorates, herniates, and or breaks down, leading to pain. There may be weakness, numbness, and pain that radiates down my legs. Sometimes, it feels like I'm standing on a burning hot coal fire. I've had four surgery consultations over the years, but I'm not a candidate for surgery. I can't get any relief from the pain, at least when it comes to surgery.

Unfortunately, as part of the treatment plan for my disability, I have to take pain medicine, and most are opioids. It's the only way I can get some relief from the pain, but I hate taking them. My behavior has changed. I've stopped yawning, and I haven't sneezed in years. I rarely move in bed during the night. All because of taking those dang opioids.

The remarkable gift and my journey through my adult life are intertwined. I don't remember ever seeing a UFO as a child. My first sighting of a UFO was in 1975 when I was 19 years old. It was right before my first marriage while I was night fishing with my then-girlfriend. The last sighting, so far, was in 2019 when I was 63 years old. I was outside on my patio with my third and last wife when a swarm of UFO orbs showed up. I have had many UFO sightings between these two encounters, including many friends and family members. That's why I say the gift and life are intertwined.

I would have been happy without the gift, but someone somewhere decided that I needed to carry this honor. Don't get me

INTRODUCTION TO THE GIFT

wrong; this is an extraordinary benefaction, and I would gracelessly thank the being that gave this to me. But some people would not call this an excellent gift but a terrifying weight. I don't see this as a burden; on the contrary, I love seeing UFOs. Any amount, any design of UFO, which is just fine with me. But does this gift make me unique? I don't think so. A life with UFOs is an honor, and I'm enjoying every minute of it!

But I've always wondered if I'm unique. Have others in the world been bestowed this gift too? Most people in the world have not witnessed any UFOs, so why me? And for that matter, most books about UFO sightings usually detail only one UFO encounter, surely not 20 separate UFO sightings! Very rarely have I found a book about multiple sightings of UFOs. But I'm still looking, searching Google or any place where I might find someone else that is just like me.

My life journey started in Maplewood, Minnesota, a suburb of St. Paul, in 1956. My childhood was somewhat OK and, in some ways, not. I say OK because I have ADHD. That's Attention Deficit Hyperactivity Disorder. I was an extremely active child. This was difficult for my parents to deal with, especially my father, a very strict and impatient parent. On the other hand, my mother was much more patient with me and tried to help me in any way she could.

My father, Ray Sr. passed away from a heart attack when he was only 51 years old. He was doing his daily 3-mile walk to stay in shape if you can believe that. Talk about a tragic irony. My mother, Jacky, also passed away but from liver problems in 2012. She was 82 years old and a good mom.

Thank God I had understanding friends, though! If it weren't for them, I surely would have been an extremely depressed kid. I was happy being with my friends because they were a bunch of crazy guys, and we did everything together.

INTRODUCTION TO THE GIFT

Doctors knew a lot about ADHD in 1964 and tried to slow me down with drugs. They would prescribe medicines like Ritalin, which is a stimulant used to treat attention deficit hyperactivity disorder. I also suffered from seizures in third grade and had to take Dilantin. It prevented me from going into convulsions, which I did in class once.

And, the wiring in my brain seemed different than most peoples. I was chemically imbalanced. What makes an ordinary person hyper like too much coffee had the opposite effect on me. Doctors needed something more substantial than Ritalin to slow me down, so they prescribed Dexedrine, a potent amphetamine. Addicts would steal this drug to get high. They would call the drug Black Dex or Black Beauties or refer to it as Speed. As you can imagine, I got addicted to it. When I was in 7th grade, my mom decided I should get off of all the medications. I went cold turkey and went through drug withdrawals — profuse sweating, chills, and vomiting for a few days. It was a hard life in the beginning, but prayers got me through it.

That's why I say I had an OK childhood. With all that was going on in my life, I had a relatively happy childhood despite being ADHD.

We were a typically sizeable Catholic family, with eight of us sharing a three-bedroom 1300 square foot house. Back then, families were much larger than they are today. Our home was one block away from the church, the Presentation of the Blessed Virgin Mary. My five crazy friends also came from large Catholic families.

With eight people crammed in a small 3-bedroom house, life wasn't that enjoyable at times. There was constant raucous and bickering, and there was no place to hide. I have three older sisters and one older brother. For 12 1/2 years, I was the baby of the family. I have a little sister that came along, stopping my rein as the baby of

INTRODUCTION TO THE GIFT

the family. Which got me mad at the time, but as adults, we're now friends. I couldn't say that when I was 12.

After 17 years of living with mom, dad, and my other siblings, I needed to get out and become independent. With little financial choices, I decided to join the military in 1974 during the Vietnam War. Not only to improve me but because I wanted to honor my uncle Bill Huberty, my mom's younger brother, who was also a Vietnam Veteran.

On October 10th, 1965, at only 18 years young, my uncle Bill was killed in Vietnam, trying to defuse landmines. The dog he had with him that was trying to locate the landmines by sniffing them out stepped on it. Unfortunately, the explosion killed him and three other men. Mom was tremendously worried about him before he left for Vietnam. That's because she foretold of his death in a dream she had.

Instead of joining the Army or Marines, I joined the Air Force. Basic training was at Lackland Air Force Base in San Antonio, Texas, for eight weeks. I surely wasn't going to join the Army as my Uncle Bill had. I was praying for orders to keep me in the states and not go to Vietnam. I received my orders after basic training and, as luck would have it, was permanently stationed at Davis-Monthan Air Force Base in Tucson, Arizona, for the entire war, and that wasn't so bad. At least no one was going to be shooting at me.

With no jungles to forge through and zero-gun fire, I was reasonably happy living on base. What's interesting about Davis-Monthan is it's the location of the 309th Aerospace Maintenance and Regeneration Group (AMARG). The sole aircraft boneyard and parts reclamation facility for all excess military and government aircraft.

There are acres upon acres of old jets, planes, and helicopters just sitting there collecting dust. Old airplanes and helicopters that are still in service sometimes need parts. If they're not manufactured anymore, they will take those parts from one sitting in the boneyard.

I have always loved jets and helicopters and any other aircraft type as far back as I can remember. One day, I thought that maybe I could go inside a plane and have a peek. I wanted to sit in the captain's chair inside the cockpit and have a little fun. There was no one guarding the gates to the boneyard, so I thought it would be a perfect time to have a look around. Sometimes there would be military police driving around the dirt streets between the jets, but it was lunchtime, and I didn't see anyone around. What a great opportunity, I thought. So, I snuck into the boneyard where the aircraft was and went inside one, a punishable offense. While having fun at the controls, the next thing I knew, I had a gun barrel pressed up to the back of my head with a guy saying, "What are you doing in here, boy?" The man holding the rifle was the military police. He escorted me out of the boneyard with no problems and no punishment. I thought that was nice of the guy. I could have lost a stripe for that, but instead, he let me go.

My title and training in the Air Force made me a Fuels Specialist, a person who has a working knowledge of jet fuel creation and bulk storage — or even pumping gas at the officer's gas station on base.

The Air Force could have had me doing any one of those jobs at any time. The position also allowed me to fuel aircraft, which I did. I was thrilled that my job was to fuel jets. They trained me to know how to fuel all aircraft types, be it fighter, bomber, and attack jets flown at the base. I was also responsible for fueling helicopters, such as the Huey Helicopter. Hueys were heavily used in the Vietnam war to either drop off troops or pick up the wounded. And to bring supplies to the troops.

And part of my training required me to fuel very sensitive jets, so I had to get a higher security clearance to perform that task. My

INTRODUCTION TO THE GIFT

job as a Fuels Specialist then narrowed to spy planes and other sensitive aircraft because of that increased security clearance. As part of those credentials, I was also part of the team fueling President Gerald Ford's airplane, Air Force One, in 1974. I remember he came to Tucson for a rally or something. Not many people can fuel the president's plane because of its sensitivity. I also fueled two spy planes, the SR-71 Blackbird and the U-2 Dragon Lady.

These are the two spy planes I used to refuel.

These jets are known today as Black Projects, which are highly secretive. I couldn't tell anyone at home that I was fueling these, nor could I take any pictures of them either. Although I did take a Polaroid picture of one after I was done refueling it and sent it to my mom. The CIA flew both jets for photographic missions over other countries. We needed to take photos of the missile capabilities in those countries and other sensitive targets for our military strategies. This was the only way for us to ensure our military superiority because satellites could not take good enough images of the ground at that time.

Some of you might remember the international incident that involved the U-2 jet. On May 1st, 1960, a United States U-2 spy plane was shot down by the Soviet Air Defense Forces while performing photographic aerial reconnaissance deep into Soviet territory. The single-seat aircraft, flown by pilot Francis Gary Powers, was hit by an S-75 Dvina surface-to-air missile and crashed near Sverdlovsk,

U.S.S.R. The pilot survived, thank goodness. The Russians could have seen this as an act of war. It caused quite an uproar. The other jet, the SR-71 Blackbird, was made to replace the U-2 because of this incident and is still the highest flying and fastest aircraft on the planet.

Unfortunately, after just ten months and 13 days of being in the Air Force, I applied for an early out. Since the military was getting out of Vietnam, there was an overabundance of personnel that needed to go back home, so they created an early out program. Anyone could apply for early out status. I won't go into the details of why I wanted to leave the job that I truly loved. I'll just say that my superiors' mindset had clashed with mine, and I became disillusioned at the prospect of staying in the military. I was granted an early out and earned an honorable discharge with honorable conditions from the U.S. Air Force in 1974, and I was only 18 at the time.

After returning from the service, I moved back to Maplewood, Minnesota, and again in with my parents. I would go down to the local bowling alley, the Maplewood Bowl, near mom and dad's house to enjoy a few beers after work. There were a few people at the bowling alley that were also Vietnam vets. I would have a few drinks with them, and we would play a little pool together, which I thoroughly enjoyed.

There was one particular waitress at the Maplewood bowl that always seemed to serve me drinks. Her name was Roxanne Cleveland, and we got along wonderfully. She was a beautiful person inside and out, and we had a lot of fun together. After getting to know her, I became smitten. I don't think it was more than a week of me going there, and I asked her out. I didn't have much money back then, so we had a few free drinks at the bowling alley on our first date.

Afterward, she suggested we go down to her mom's house in Cottage Grove, MN, and have some fun playing pool in their basement. That's when I met her family. They were all quite different and somewhat strange people, and I knew right then that I wanted to be with this kind of family. I was also slightly different than most people, and we all got along nicely. I came to love them all very much.

After about two months, Roxanne moved out of her mom's house and into an apartment near the Maplewood Bowl. We kept dating and having a lot of fun together. We would go back to her apartment and have a few more drinks and talk. Roxy and I would talk late into the night. She was a joy and an easy-going person, and I loved being with her. I have fond memories of us drinking and laughing at her apartment.

Roxy's family was somewhat large, too, with five members in all. Roxanne's mother, Bonnie, was a single mom and doing a great job at raising the family. Her husband Charles, unfortunately, had passed away at 42 from a brain aneurysm. She had an older brother Greg, a younger sister Tammie and a younger brother, Brian, who was also the baby of the family like me.

It was about three months after I met Roxanne that I asked her if it would be OK to move in with her. She was renting a 1-bedroom apartment. I was staying at dad's house, and this was not where I wanted to be anymore. Roxanne said it would be OK if I moved in with her, which I did.

Once I knew she was the one, I thought, hey, why not. I knew I wanted to spend the rest of my life with her. We got along so very well that I asked her to marry me in 1976. We both were unusually young. I was just 19, and Roxanne was 20.

After a couple of years of living together in this one-bedroom apartment, we were expecting our first child. In 1978 our son, Tony was born. Requiring more space and not wanting to waste money with apartment living, we purchased a townhome in a suburb of

INTRODUCTION TO THE GIFT

St. Paul, Minnesota, called Oakdale. We enjoyed our lives together there, and in 1983 our last-child, Steven, was born.

I wrote the book a little differently than how other non-fiction books are written. The first eight chapters are in chronological order from my first sighting of a UFO in 1975 until my last sighting in 2015. Each of these first eight chapters will be about a major sighting, which is an actual ship, or multiple ships where I can define their characteristics. The ninth or last chapter is only about minor UFO sightings like star-like objects. The sightings of these star-like objects intertwine between and after the major sightings, and that's why I put them in a separate section.

The next chapter is about when and where my gift started, and it began with a bang. As part of the marriage with Roxanne, her family owned a cabin in Cumberland, Wisconsin. That's where I saw my first UFO, and it was terrifying!

1

UFO over Pipe Lake

"Behind the scenes, high-ranking Air Force officers are soberly concerned about UFOs. But through official secrecy and ridicule, many citizens are led to believe that unknown flying objects are nonsense."
Roscoe Hillenkoetter,
Former CIA Director, public statement, 1960.

When I was younger, I never thought I would have seen a UFO ever in my wildest dreams or would be entangled with them somehow. How and why the universe chose me for this glorious life with UFOs is beyond me. But I am eternally grateful for the gift that has been bestowed on me. And having the people I love involved with my UFO sightings only adds to my joy. If it were only me seeing these UFOs, I would have thought I was crazy, but including other witnesses with me has made me feel less insane and has added some credibility to my sightings.

I'm a baby boomer and was born in 1956. When Neil Armstrong and Buzz Aldrin stepped on the moon, my entire family sat in front of the television, amazed at what was happening. I had had just turned 13 and was very impressionable at that time. I wondered back then if there was life in other places in the universe. I also wondered if they have visited us and some kid on their planet was watching a show and seeing his or her people step out on Earth for the first time.

My fifth-grade teacher nurtured me with thoughts of a universe beyond what I could see around me. He had a small astronomy club and asked me to join. The very first object I saw in that telescope of his was Saturn and those beautiful rings. Reading about the planets is one thing but seeing them in a telescope was thrilling. My mind opened to all sorts of faraway thoughts about life on distant planets and maybe visitors to our world. I didn't have to wait long for my dreams to come true.

In 1975, my wife Roxanne and I had started to go to her mom's cabin on Pipe Lake near the little farming community of Cumberland, Wisconsin. Her parents, Bonnie and Charles, purchased the cabin before her dad's passing. It was only about 110 miles northeast of St. Paul, Minnesota, a leisurely drive for weekend excursions. It was in Polk County, which is a part of west-central Wisconsin.

It wasn't large or fancy in any way, but I loved going up there because it wasn't home. I had never gone to a cabin on a lake before, and it was where I needed to be. I had a stressful managerial position at a retail store. And I needed some well-deserved R & R. It was a tiny and very moldy smelling 2-bedroom cabin with an open kitchen, dinette, and living room area. If the whole place were more than 600 square feet, I would be surprised, but I still cherished it.

It sat on a densely wooded area on top of an incredibly steep hill overlooking Pipe Lake. There were White and Red Oaks, Poplars, and Pine trees everywhere. Trees lining the roads and trees all over the land near the cabin. I guess you could consider it an old-growth forest because most of the trees were large and mature.

Bonnie's cabin overlooking Pipe Lake.

It was an ideal place for water skiing or being dragged on an inner-tube behind a boat because Pipe Lake is 1.5 miles long and just a couple of hundred yards wide. You could water-ski until your arms got weary, which we achieved on many occasions. It also helps to have a neighbor with skiing equipment and a speed boat. Pipe Lake offered a lot of outdoor activities, and our family enjoyed them all for years.

And Oh My God, the water was so clear! I could see the bottom of the lake in 25 feet of water. The Department of Natural Resources classified Pipe Lake as one of the clearest lakes in all of Wisconsin some years ago.

All through the years, we would go fishing, swimming, and walking through the woods. And the kids and I especially loved going through the woods together. Oh, the many questions they would ask me about this and that. I loved every inquiry!

There was also a 10-foot by the 10-foot floating dock about 40 feet or so from our shoreline. That made it a leisurely swim for my oldest boy Tony to get there. Steven, our youngest child, would always want to do what his older brother did, so I had to help him swim to the dock. Steven used to get earaches from swimming because he would get water in them, which also contained bacteria. He got earaches at least every other week. So, we had to put a little white swimming cap on his head to protect his ears from getting water in them. I felt so sorry for him during that time. The floating dock was shared with two other cabins making it a lot easier to bring to shore at summers end.

This is where the gift started and with a bang. The year we witnessed the UFO was in 1975. I'm not confident what the exact date was, but sometime in the fall of that year. My birthday is in May, so I know I was 19 years old then. At that time, I could not have imagined I would have a life with UFOs. Throughout my childhood and just starting adulthood, I had never seen a UFO. When this sighting happened, though, it completely transformed my life. And it changed the people that were with me too.

Sometime during the early fall of '75, Roxanne suggested that we go to the cabin to do some fishing. Since we were babysitting her younger brother Brian, she suggested we take him up there because Brian enjoyed fishing. So I asked him if he wanted to go and he said yes. We all got in my 1974 white Chevy Nova and drove to Pipe Lake. Roxy and I didn't have kids back then, so we were relatively free to do what we wanted when we wanted.

My brother-in-law, Brian, was a little chubby and sweet kid. Well, he was a little more than chubby, he was an adult-sized 13-year-old kid. We clicked almost immediately. Yea, he was a kid, but I felt like we were kindred spirits. Both of us were the babies of the family and somewhat tormented by our siblings as children. Especially our older brothers. To this day, Brian and I are best friends. We have done a lot of things together and have many things in common. I enjoy his company because he's the little brother I never had.

Before we got to the cabin, we stopped at a bait store. We needed to get some fresh bait like minnows, leeches, and worms that the fish we were about to catch like to eat. After about an hour and a half, we finally made it to the cabin later in the evening. We unpacked the car and brought in a cooler of beer and food and the bait. I was looking forward to catching some fishing.

It wasn't more than ten minutes after we unpacked and put everything away Roxanne said, "Hey, does anyone want to get some night fishing in before it gets too late?" Usually, I wouldn't have gone fishing then because it was very late in the evening, but something was drawing me to the lake. This was early in the fall, and most of the cabins had been shut down for the season. No one was around if something went wrong out on the lake so we wouldn't have had anyone to help us get back to the shore. It was a dumb idea and a bit risky, but I got this all-consuming feeling of needing to get out on the water.

Roxy, Brian, and I gathered the gear and bait to do night fishing and catch some walleyes. These are freshwater fish native to most of Canada and the northern United States. They are fish that primarily hunts for other fish at night and they love leeches, and nightcrawlers or what you might call worms, and that's why I bought them. Fishing for walleyes is a lot of fun, and Brian was more than ready.

One hugely successful way of catching nighttime walleyes is trolling for them. Trolling from a boat involves moving quite slowly through the water. I accomplished this with the use of my electric trolling motor. Multiple lines are frequently employed, and outriggers can spread the lines more widely, plus it reduces the chance of tangling. Or getting caught in the prop of the main engine.

Walleyes usually hang out near a sandy area and have been known to like rocky lake bottoms too. That's what so great about Pipe Lake. It has both those types of places to fish. Most of the time, when I would go fishing, I would come back with a walleye or two.

Back then, I owned a small 14-foot aluminum boat and an electric trolling motor connected to a car battery at the back of the craft. The main engine was an old low power Evinrude 10 horsepower motor. When you include two adults and one large child in a small boat like this, it would stress that Evinrude motor out. Not to mention that little electric trolling motor too. The Evinrude motor was strong and reliable, but it was easier to propel only one person in the boat, not three adult-sized people. I thought, what the heck, let's try it out anyway and see how well this boat will move.

We grabbed everything we needed from the cabin, including three fishing poles, leeches, worms, and sodas for us to enjoy. I grabbed the cooler of beer so that I could enjoy the fishing too. We made our way outside but not looking forward to bringing all the gear down the steep hill.

Trying to walk down that precipitous hill, at night, with no lights for guidance, with all the gear was difficult at best. You could have all the flashlights in the world, but that still wouldn't help walking down that hill at night any more manageable. I stumbled a couple of times with the heavy cooler, but we finally made it to the dock and we were all ready to catch some fish.

We got to the boat, through everything inside, untied it from the dock, and away we went. You know, it wasn't that bad. The little Evinrude worked pretty well with all of us in it. I shut off the engine and started using the electric trolling motor because we were in walleye territory, a sandy lake bottom, and needed to be quieter.

I was enjoying myself looking up at the stars. I was paying more attention to them and my beer than I was fishing. The night was so clear, and the stars were shining like diamonds. I've always loved looking at the stars at the cabin. It makes one get poetic and somewhat philosophical.

We had just rounded the south side of the lake not far from the dock where the sandy public beach is when something happened. I was controlling the trolling motor and looking north down the lake at the stars. Roxanne was on my right facing east, and Brian was on my left facing west. Once I got past the beach area, Roxy yelled out, "Hey, Ray! What's that over there?" I looked at her and saw that she was pointing towards something up in the air.

I jacked my head up, right where Roxanne was pointing, and there it was. A ball of flames and it was rising. I was stunned! I said, what the...? What the hell is that thing, Roxanne? Brian immediately turned around because he had his back to this thing. We were all staring at it, and I think all of us were stunned at that point because no one said anything.

As we all looked where Roxanne was pointing, we saw the flames just above the tree line, so it had to be about 75 to maybe 100 feet or so off the ground. And I estimate that the ball of fire was only about 75 to perhaps 100 yards away, which was close enough for me. I didn't want it to come any closer than that. I did a quick edit in my mind right then and believed it to be around 40 - 50 feet in diameter. I was thinking, holy crap, that thing is enormous! To me, that's a massive ball of flames, especially since there should not be any flames rising out of the woods anyway. Providing that's where it came from because I don't think anyone was sure at that moment. I know I wasn't.

The flames could have come out from either a wooded area or the lake's access road, which weaves through the forest. It most likely came from the road because the road snakes through the forest before it finally reaches the beach. Knowing exactly where the road goes through the forest is an impossible trick because of all the curves.

Ariel view of Pipe Lake. The red star is where we were fishing, and the orange object is the location of the Fireball UFO.

Since the flames were maybe 100 yards away, they were somewhat indistinguishable from a ball because of the distance. I was thinking, was this just a ball of fire, or was it something else. When I say it was a ball of fire, one thing was for sure. It was a very bright red and orange color, and it seemed like the shape was round.

It was rising slowly but surely out of what I believed at the time was the forest, but how could that be? It then dawned on me. No, it can't be coming out of the woods, Ray, because if it did, it would have surely started a fire. It had to have been on the access road.

I didn't have a pair of binoculars, and of course, in 1975, there were no cell phones with their excellent cameras either. So everything I am describing here was from the memory of Roxy, Brian, and me.

We were all dumbfounded. I remember my hand dropped off the trolling motor's throttle, and we started to coast through the water. I could see that Roxy and Brian had their fishing poles in their laps, just transfixed on this object. I must have also dropped my rod down in the boat because I couldn't feel the pole's handle anymore.

I was getting scared because this thing was slowly rising, and I was worried it might do something. My mind was trying its hardest to identify this thing, whatever this thing was. And not only that, but where could it have come from anyway? There's no way humans could have made a ball of flames like this. Even I knew that. And that's precisely why I was so scared because I knew this thing was not from this Earth!

Roxanne looked at me and said, "What do you think that thing is, Raymond?" Brian asked me if I've ever seen anything like that, and I told him no. I said to Roxy that I think it's a hot air balloon. But then I thought that hot air balloons don't typically fly at night. Plus, there was no sound associated with this ball of flames. The burners on hot air balloons are very noisy, so I instantly dismissed that thought from my mind.

In a minute or so, we were all throwing out suggestions, and nothing would fit. Somebody said maybe someone released a Chinese lantern. But I said it couldn't be one of those because it was too big. I said it has to be at least 50 feet in diameter, and Chinese lanterns are not that large. I thought maybe someone could have lit something on fire and let it go floating away? But the thing was entirely round, so that thought was gone too.

It seemed that each of us was trying to avoid saying the "U" word, as in UFO! We were all terrified at this point. Even though the object was rising and not coming towards us, we were still petrified. At that moment, we stopped wondering what it was. We all looked at each other in utter amazement. Hey, wait a darn minute, I said. As you would expect, I did not say darn, but an expletive came out of my mouth so that I won't share the word here. OH MY GOD, ROXY – IT'S A UFO!

The instant I said those words, the thing then stopped! Then I was freaking out inside my head. Did that thing hear us and stop, I thought? Is it going to come our way and maybe abduct us? Naturally, I can't know if it heard us or saw us or not, but it did give me that impression that it did, which is why my heart was pounding in my throat!

I then looked over at Roxanne and Brian and saw absolute fear on their faces because of what I just said. I'm not sure what my expression was, but you can bet your life that it was the same look of fear because I was getting that flight or fight feeling. The fight or flight response is an automatic physiological reaction to an event that is perceived as stressful or frightening. The perception of threat triggers an acute stress response that prepares the body to fight or flee. Basically, my adrenaline was flowing through my body at the speed of light, and I wanted to get out of there pronto! I think all of us were feeling unsafe at that moment in time.

The ball of flames could have been a UFO craft, or maybe it was a red and orange UFO orb of some kind, but either way, I knew it was some kind of UFO and not from here. I don't know where it came from and hoped I would never see one of these again. I'm sure that goes for my passengers too.

We were all tremendously horrified because it was considerably late, and we were all alone in that little boat, and that's not where we wanted to be anymore. I was thinking of screaming for help. There were cabins close to us, but none of their lights were on. And I was thinking how weird it is because of the dead silence. There was no wind, and everything felt eerie.

On the other side of the access road across from the beach, there's a farm, and usually, there are cows out, but we heard nothing from them. Which only added to my fears. There was no traffic anywhere on the road—just complete and utter silence.

I was thinking that if a UFO could have come down on the street, did whatever UFOs do, and was taking off, maybe if it would please just take off, I wouldn't have to worry anymore. I didn't know what to do. I am not exactly sure how long the UFO hovered in the air, but it was long enough for the other occupants of that little boat and me.

As my heart was thumping out of my chest, the boat came to a slow and gentle stop. Our lines were still in the water, but I wasn't thinking about the fishing lines or fishing or trolling for that matter. The only thing I was thinking was I have to get out of there and do it quickly!

We were all mesmerized by this ball of flames. I have never witnessed anything like it in my entire life, and I'm confident you would agree with me that I needed to do something and fast. I possessed an overwhelming feeling of needing to protect my family. I thought, why am I just sitting here in this little boat in pitch-black darkness with no help from anyone else? And maybe being abducted, I thought. Shouldn't it be prudent for me to protect my brother-in-law Brian and wife Roxy from harm? So, that's what I did.

Roxanne started screaming, "Let's go, let's go, let's go. Let's get out of here, Raymond. Come On, Come On!" Roxanne has a good head on her shoulder and is an extremely strong woman. She's been by herself for a long time and has taken care of things that would put most people to shame. She's been through a lot. And I have never seen her like this, feeling utterly defenseless and completely terrified. This was the first and only time I had ever heard Roxanne scream or be that frightened. Her screaming only made me feel panic-stricken at what we were seeing.

You have to remember something. It was 1975, and way before UFOs were more of a mainstream subject matter. In today's world, UFOs are mentioned on the TV at least once a month. That goes with newspapers too. You can read about someone seeing a UFO almost every time you pick one up, it seems.

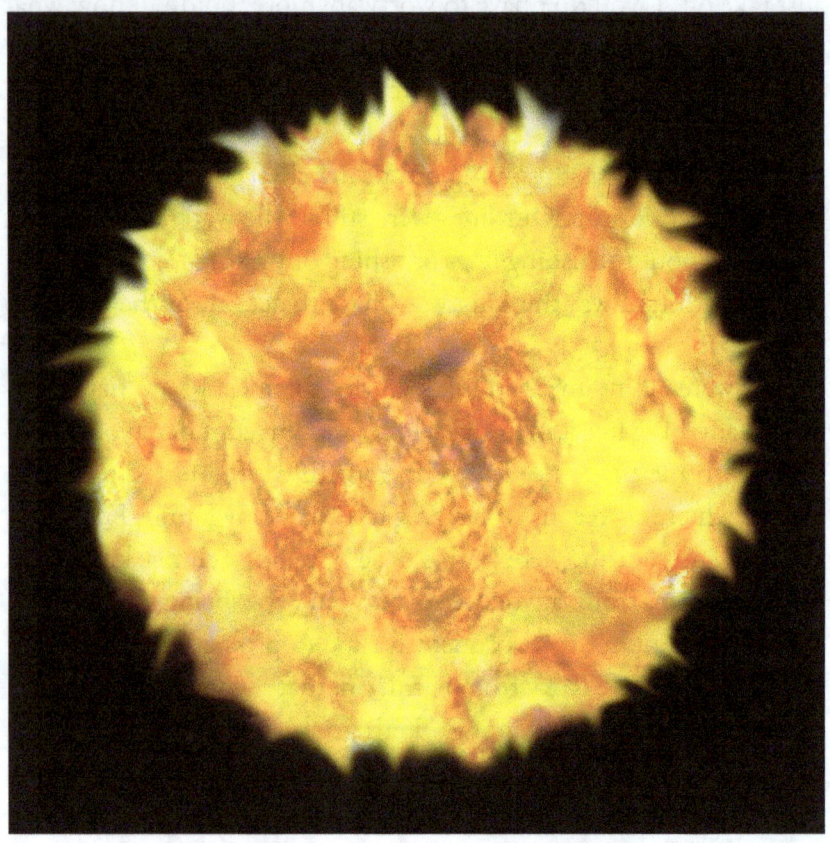

This is exactly what we witnessed while fishing.

This was a rare situation we were in, and nobody I had ever known had ever witnessed a UFO before. It was all fine and good that we were the first to see a UFO, but I would have chosen to be farther down the list of someone witnessing one.

I was so terrified that I pulled on the rope of that motor as hard as possible to get it started. I thought I was going to snap the cord because I pulled it so hard. It usually takes a couple of pulls to get the engine started, but luck would have it, I got it going on one good frightened tug.

I ordered everyone to reel their lines back in, so we can take off. If we didn't reel the fishing lines back in, they could have spun around the motor's prop or blades, and we would have stalled right there in the middle of the lake. I managed to get my line back in the boat quickly. Then I turned the throttle handle of that little 10-horsepower motor as hard as I could to get us going. All I could think of was wanting to get back to the cabin where we'll all be safe.

I looked over at Brian, and he looked horrified while he was reeling his line back in. He was crying by then, and I felt so sorry for him. Between his tears, he and Roxy were screaming at me. I wasn't sure what they were saying, but whatever it was, it was loud! And that wasn't helping me. It was only getting me more afraid. I remember my hands were shaking like hummingbird wings as I tried to keep my hand on the throttle.

You know when you're so terrified, doesn't it seem like time slows down? To me, it felt like an eternity. I was in some slow-motion picture and could not get back to the dock fast enough. The dock was only a hundred yards or so away, but it felt like forever to get there. Most likely, it was only a minute or so, but that minute was long enough for me.

We finally reached the dock, and I was overjoyed. Actually, the front of the boat slammed into the shore next to the dock. Roxy and Brian jumped out of the boat and onto the dock. Since I was in the back of the boat, this made me farthest from the shore. I jumped out of the boat and landed knee-high into the water. I forced my way, trudging through the water, like going through wet cement and finally reaching the beach. I don't know why, but they were trying to get stuff out of the boat. I screamed, don't grab anything from the boat. Let's just get up the hill. We looked like cockroaches scrambling around in the light.

The cabin is on top of an incredibly steep hill making things worse. There were no stairs or lights to assist us, so we had to climb up the hill as best we could to get to the cabin. Roxy and I made it all right, but poor little Brian was slipping on the wet grass and needed assistance. Roxy turned around and went down to get him. We ultimately got to the place, and we all ran inside. We were all out of breath from racing up the hill and were panting like overheated dogs.

Brian shot straight back to the rear bedroom. I am not sure if he hid under the bunk beds or the blankets, but there he stayed, at least for a while. Brian had just turned 14, and I felt extremely sorry for him. I'm sure witnessing a ball of flames traumatized the poor kid, and it didn't help me calling it a UFO. Well, what kid wouldn't have the daylights scared out of him at the site of one of those things.

Roxy looked at me and said, "Raymond, what WAS that thing? Do you think it's following us? Where did it come from, Raymond? Are we going to be safe in the cabin, or should we get in the car and go back home?"

Brian must have heard her because he came out of the back bedroom. He shouted, "I just want to go back home, Roxy! Can we please go back home?" Then he started begging me. "Please, Ray, I don't want to be here anymore. Can we please go back home, please?" They asked me all sorts of questions like I knew what was going on, but I was just as ill-informed as they.

What could I say? What should we do? Should we stay here, and maybe this thing will come to the cabin? I was just as lost and just as confused as they were. I was trying to put on my best face and look as strong as a man should be. But inside, I was shaking to death and panic-stricken. I knew I needed to be strong for them. That was my job, and I was going to do it admirably. Well, as good as I could, given the circumstances. That was the first time I felt scared and bewildered and so vulnerable I wanted to scream. I know that what I'm about to say might sound sexist, but back then, it wasn't. It is my job as Roxanne's husband to protect and defend her and Brian with my life, and that is what I would have done if it had gotten to that point, but thank the Lord it didn't.

I said, Roxanne, I just don't know what that thing was, honey. I do know that it seemed to rise, then it stopped when we said the UFO word. But I'm not quite sure if it saw us or not. I asked her, do you think it saw us? She said "I hope not!" I told her that I looked back at it when we got to the dock. And I saw it rising again, so no, I don't think it's coming after us. I'm going to have a couple of beers first to calm my nerves, then go back down to the dock. Roxanne was like, "NO WAY RAYMOND, NO WAY MAN! I don't want you abducted or whatever. Just stay up here for a little while longer, please, then you can go back down to the dock and see if you see it because I know you want to. Come on, dude, please stay here with me for a while!"

After quickly pounding a couple of beers, I slowly headed back down the hill. I was looking up and around all over the place. I wanted to make sure it wasn't above or near me. I finally made it down the hill and to the dock but not all the way out. All I could muster was about halfway out. I was sliding my left foot forward a little with each step. I wasn't that brave quite yet. OK, I don't see it, I thought and crept farther and farther out looking everywhere. My head was jerking around like a bobblehead toy trying to figure out just exactly where it was. But I couldn't see the UFO anymore. The fireball UFO was gone entirely, and I was relieved and saddened at the same time. My first UFO, and it was nowhere to be seen.

Once I knew it was finally gone, I stood there on the dock and looked up, staring at the stars. Yea, I was still scared, but yet I could finally reflect on what all this was. I never witnessed anything like this before and thought I just squandered a chance in a lifetime.

I had witnesses, but no concrete proof beyond that. We had only the memories but no photo. My family and I were safe, so why all the freaking out? It never made any threatening moves towards us. We could have remained in the boat and enjoy the show. But was I that brave? Uh, NO I wasn't!

Unfortunately, witnessing a slow rising ball of flames while feeling unprepared and unprotected in a tiny boat doesn't allow a person much time to determine what it was, exactly. Where did it come up from, the forest or the road? And where was it going? And maybe what kind of alien could be inside navigating this ship? I guess I'll never know the answers, but I indeed wanted to find out.

It made no sound, which in itself was a spooky feeling. Wouldn't you think you would hear some noise from a ball of flames, though? Campfires make popping noises. Even a lighter has a slight whoosh to it. And what was on fire anyway? I was glad the UFO was by itself, and there weren't any other UFOs. One was enough for me.

After seeing it was positively gone, I went back up to the cabin. I told Roxy that everything was OK, and it was gone. She asked me, "Raymond, should we leave? What if that thing comes back?" I told her that we'd be alright, and the incident is over. We don't have to worry anymore.

Brian must have returned to the back bedroom because I didn't see him once I got back to the cabin. Both Roxy and I went into the back bedroom where Brian was. We went to console him as best as we could. He was on the lower bunk bed, squeezed way back in the corner with the blankets pulled up past his nose. All I could see was his eyes peeking out of the blankets, and they were as round as two white cue balls. And he was still so scared and shaking.

I'm not sure what his questions were, but I do know he was firing off one after another about what just happened. We tried to console him as best we could and assure him that the fireball was gone and would never come back. Roxy and I were doing everything we could NOT using the UFO word because we knew it would set him off again. It took about an hour of reassurance until he finally settled down enough to come out of the room back to the kitchen.

Roxy and I didn't say too much after that, so Brian would want to stay at the cabin and keep fishing. As far as I remember, we all enjoyed the rest of our weekend fishing and swimming. None of us have ever spoken of that night until I was writing this book. Brian is still horrified to this day about that night.

I realize that witnessing something so out of the ordinary can be alarming, but sometimes you can get awestruck too, as I was with this next sighting. I absolutely couldn't believe what my eyes were seeing. I was fishing with my son Steven on the Mississippi River. It transformed Steven so entirely that wanting to see another UFO is now paramount in his life. The following chapter is an up-close and personal type of sighting, too, because these UFOs were much closer to us than the one at the cabin.

2

2 UFOs Over the Mississippi

"The astonishing thing would be if they did not exist."
Jean Cocteau.

As the '70s rolled on and into the 1980s, there were no other UFO encounters. Roxanne and I divorced in 1988. We decided that she keep the children, and we agreed that I could pick them up and be with them every other weekend. If there was some type of function that required one kid or the other in the middle of the weeks, she was all too happy to let me see them. We were still friends, and we had an amicable agreement on raising the boys.

It wasn't that I didn't love Roxy. The truth be told, I didn't want to be married to a white woman — something I acquired when I was 13 years young. At my 7th grade dance, I met a cute little African American girl. We went behind the curtains of the stage to be away from prying eyes and kissed and talked. She was the first girl I ever kissed, and I loved it! I thought she was beautiful, and I couldn't get enough. The year was 1969, just five years after the Civil Rights Movement, and people were afraid to integrate but not me. After the dance, I asked her to be my girlfriend, but she was scared of what her father might think. I suggested she ask him anyway, and let's see what he would say. She talked to her father the next day, and he absolutely forbid it. As her father said to her, "You ain't dating no white boy!" So that was that, and it broke my heart. But we stayed friends until I transferred to another school in 9th grade and never saw her again.

I had never had trouble with other people. Especially people of color. None of my family did. Our parents raised us to look at others as human beings and not look at their skin color. A person's worth was in their words, not on their skin. My older sister dated a friendly black kid, Dez Dickerson, the lead guitar player for the band Prince. At a very young age, we were taught not to discriminate against anyone based on race, creed, color, ethnicity, national origin, religion, sex, sexual orientation, gender expression, no matter who they were, PERIOD! I grew up with black friends and gay friends, so I knew better. I have always looked at African-American women as some of the most beautiful creatures on earth. I am currently married to a black woman.

During the late stages of my marriage to Roxy, I was getting more and more disillusioned with each passing year. I remember that sometime after my first son Tony was born, I didn't want to be married to a white woman anymore. I held my feelings deep inside me as long as I could because I didn't want to hurt Roxanne. I carried those feelings for years and years. Another big reason I stayed so long despite what I felt was that I didn't want to leave my children. So, I had to wait and wait until I couldn't wait anymore. I had to be true to myself and my feelings, and unfortunately, I asked Roxanne for a divorce.

My job at that time was selling heating and air conditioning at Sedgwick Heating in Minneapolis. I was a very successful salesman and decided to start my own business. It was named Innovative Heating and Air, Inc. I sold heating and cooling products to homeowners and builders of new house construction and remodeling contractors.

I got the company up and running while spending as much time with the kids as I could. I did my best, but it was hard, as you can imagine. Unfortunately, I couldn't spend too much time with the boys because I had to work 100+ hours a week to get a new business going. Although they have never complained about me not spending that much time with them, I knew they weren't truly happy.

To make some extra money for the business, I would take the old A/C units and furnaces I replaced from people's homes to a Junkyard/Recycling plant. It's was a great way to make extra money and to help the environment. The units needed weighing to determine just how much there is of recycled metal for payment. We made a lot of money in recycling those units.

One day, in 1989, when I went to the Northern Metal Recycling plant, there was an attractive woman as the scale operator weighing the items brought in for recycling. We sparked up a conversation and instantly hit it off. She was a wonderful and beautiful person, I thought. Her name was Christina, and she was an African American, exactly what I wanted. She was about ten years younger than me and was a lot of fun. Christina was a small, 135-pound woman with long legs and dark skin, and I couldn't have wished for more.

I asked her out, and we went to a local R&B (Rhythm and Blues) club. She seemed more mature than her age, and we had some great conversations. She also loved to dance and drink and drink and dance. I didn't know it at the time, but this was going to haunt me.

But I was going through a midlife crisis and wanted to let my hair down, as it were. I used to drive a Chevy Caprice family car but purchased a new red Chevy T-Top Camaro after the divorce. Midlife crisis strikes again.

She and Roxanne were polar-opposites. And this was exactly what I was looking for in a woman. Christina and I dated for a year and a half, and I asked her to marry me. Neither of us wanted a church wedding, so we made plans to have a Las Vegas one. In 1991 we flew to Las Vegas, Nevada, and tied the knot. It was not like my first marriage. We argued a lot about her drinking, but since there were no other red flags, I was hoping she would curb her appetite for it so we could be a little happier. You pick your battles in all relationships trying to make a better life for each other.

Christina was somewhat of a tomboy and loved to do things outdoors. We would go fishing at some of the numerous lakes in Minnesota. I couldn't get her to stop fishing because she cherished it so much. We would go all over the St. Paul metropolitan area catching every kind of fish there were. She was very squeamish at putting the bait on the hook, and once she caught a fish, she just could not get herself to take it off. That was left up to me to do, I guess. But we still loved going to different parks and fishing together.

It was now the early 1990s. I'm not exactly sure what the year was for this next sighting, but I think it was during the fall of 1993. The very first UFO I experienced in 1975 seemed but a vague memory. I saw no more UFOs through the '80s, but believe me, when I say, I looked everywhere. I was hoping against hope that there was going to be a UFO in some way in some manner. That first sighting profoundly changed me and the others with me. I know I said that the UFO terrified me, but it also piqued my interest in them. All those hopes and dreams of wanting to witness another UFO finally faded as the years went by.

Since there were no other UFOs, well, what else could I do? The best answer I can give for that question is raising my children. Raising kids can be fun, and being a dad is the greatest thing a man can experience. Shaping, molding, and teaching your children can be so enjoyable. And a fulfilling experience that I couldn't get enough of, but not having both my boys with me full-time was a tremendous strain on me because I was a hands-on father. It was me who did everything with them. The kids and I would go fishing together. We would hike through the many forests in Minnesota together. They and I loved to be outdoors, and there's plenty to do outside in St. Paul.

If one of my kids wanted to be in the Cub Scouts, I would be the Cub Master. If the other wanted to play baseball, I would be the coach so both of us could have more fun together. I wanted to be there for them when and if he needed me. Oh, how wonderful it is to be a dad and to answer all those questions.

The first time I went fishing with my oldest son, Tony, was down the road from our townhome at Olsen Lake in Oakdale, Minnesota. I bought him a great little fishing rod to use. It was called the Snoopy Rod and Reel, and he treasured it. The first fish he caught was a Small Mouth Bass right from the shoreline and only after a couple of casts. You should have seen the look on his face. He had this huge smile from ear to ear after catching that fish. Olsen Lake was a nearby place to get to and a short drive from the townhome so he could enjoy some fishing.

That's Minnesota for you. We would always say; you can't take three steps backward without putting your foot in a lake. The Minnesota license plates even say, "The Land of 10,000 Lakes" on them, so you know there are many places to fish, swim, or water ski. There are, in fact, almost 22,000 lakes in all. Water sports are an excellent activity there too.

Once, while I was with my youngest son Steven and the wife Christina, we decided to go fishing on the Mississippi River. As I stated earlier, it was the fall of 1993, and Steven was close to ten years old at the time. My oldest son Tony was visiting his grandmother and wasn't able to come fishing with us.

The Mississippi River offered us some fantastic places to fish and some hidden away spots too. I can stand by myself on the shoreline, cast my line out, and maybe catch a catfish or two without other people bothering me. That's because I possess a deep affection for going to secluded places to fish. To me, it's as if I am the only person on earth at those spots. I like that feeling because if there are 40 or 50 other people all fishing simultaneously, it unnerves me, and it's a little stressing being around too many people.

Having other people around me means kids yelling, mommy, mommy, look at me! Or boats with loud engines zipping this way and that. And sometimes skiers behind those boats rushing by you, causing waves. Or the idiot on a jet-ski flying around, creating a torrent of waves in the water. I could go on, but I think you get the point.

I don't want to sound too negative; I just like being alone. Even today, if I go shopping, say at Costco or Walmart, and the parking lot is full, I want to turn right around and go back home. It has nothing to do with there being too much sound scaring the fish away. Because you can scream all you want at the water, and there will still be fish under your boat. I don't believe having too many people around is going to stop anyone from catching fish. I get anxious being around too many people, that's all.

Working as a salesperson means having to smile day in and day out while trying to convince someone to purchase your wares. Sales can be a very stressful job because you have to be an actor. And most salespeople are. We act happy, and we always have to wear a smile on our faces. We act like our products are the only product the customer should purchase even if we don't think this ourselves. I've been around a lot of salespeople, and most of them are liars. Sorry to say, but a lot of them will lie to your face to get a sale. Although I never sold an inferior product, I've always believed that giving the customer excellent service outweighed the products I sold. And I don't lie. I have always tried to tell the truth.

After a long day of work, I would look forward to those out of the way places. And one of those places I wanted to go fishing to enjoy the seclusion with my wife and son was down the Mississippi River in Inver Grove Heights, a suburb of St. Paul.

We were on the western side of the river, looking for a way to get to the shore. To get to this out of the way place for fishing, I had to travel down Concorde Avenue heading south. I finally found River Road and turned onto it to get to the Mississippi. There are many places to stop and fish off this road. As the name implies, it runs along the Mississippi River and through several cities.

As I was going down River Road, I had a strong urge to keep looking for a more secluded spot to fish. I passed many inlet roads to the river, but I just didn't feel like those were the right places to stop. I thought I had finally found an excellent spot to fish. That's because it looked quite secluded, but it didn't look like we could access the river from where we were. What I did know, though, was that I had a strong, almost overwhelming feeling that this was where we needed to be. Whatever the sensation was, it was forcing me to go there. I was trying to figure out why I was getting this all-consuming feeling that I needed to stop there and nowhere else.

So I gave into those feelings and parked the car. Christina asked me if I was sure this is where we want to fish because it didn't look like we could get access to the river. I told her it felt like a great place to be. Plus, it really looked like an out of the way too. She understood that I didn't like being around too many people and told me that it's OK, let's go here.

We got out of the car, Steven and I loaded ourselves up with the fishing gear, a few portable folding chairs, a cooler of beer and soda pops, and headed towards the river. I was looking forward to a nice relaxing day of fishing. Christina told me she was looking forward to catching some fish. Steven said, "Yea, dad, let's catch a ton of fish."

As we walked to the river, we had to go through an area strewn with bushes. Do you know how hard it can be to bring a load of gear through bushes? It's almost impossible, but somehow, something was drawing me to *this* exact spot. The road had ended at the bushes, and there wasn't a walking path through them to ease our struggle. And we were trying to walk over a lot of big rocks and debris and such. To say it was challenging is an understatement. I was questioning my decision about this place but stayed the course and trudged on. I've never been to this spot, so what was bringing me here? Fish are everywhere in the Mississippi, so why here, I wondered?

We kept digging through the brush and over tons of sticker plants to get to the river. A sticker plant has annoying tiny spikes and burrs that stick to clothing, and it's a hassle walking through them. Those stickers or burrs are the fruit of these plants. They have hooked spikes that help the fruit stick to clothing or the fur of passing animals. They can get all over a person's shoes, socks, and pants and puncture through to the skin, and it hurts. After we pushed through those almost impenetrable bushes and stickers, we finally found the Mississippi River.

I was ecstatic because when I say I wanted to be in a secluded place, you couldn't get more private than where we ended up. I didn't hear anything but the slight ringing in my ears. I looked both ways down the shoreline and found we were all alone. No boats, no jet-skis, and above all, there were no people anywhere to be seen.

Steven and I dropped all the gear and set up the folding chairs getting ready to fish. But first, Steven was yelling for me to help him take off all the stickers he got on his socks and clothes. He said, "Dad, these things are poking me in my ankles and cutting into my skin. Can you take them off of me, please?" He had tons of them all over him, which took me quite a while to remove them before we could start fishing. I had taken my stickers off a couple of minutes before.

Luckily, Christina didn't get caught up in any sticker bushes and didn't seem to need any assistance, so I went back to getting everything ready to start fishing. Christina said, "Great place Ray, but man, that was an ordeal, wasn't it?" I reminded her how I love secluded places, but I never told her about that strange feeling of needing to get to that exact spot. I now know it was the gift and that the gift started at Pipe Lake. Never in my wildest dreams could I imagine I would have a life with UFOs.

I looked across the river and wondered how strange it was that we ended up right across from the St. Paul Oil Refinery, owned by Marathon Petroleum Corporation. I didn't think we had progressed that far down the river road, but we must have. Once I ultimately saw that oil refinery, I exhaled and said a long, WHEW! I thought that this place better be worth it because once we're all done fishing, we'll have to go right back the same way and slam through those dang bushes and sticker plants again.

People in the area call the St. Paul Oil Refinery Santa's Workshop. I've used that terminology for years with the boys to help them believe that's where Santa makes all his toys. I do this so they can have a more whimsical time around Christmas.

Santa's Workshop.

It's referred to as Santa's Workshop because the plant possesses holding tanks and pipes going several hundred feet up in the air with lots of lights on top of many of the structures. And there's a huge flame that burns off excess natural gas, I assume. We would tell our kids that this was Santa's factory where he and his elves would make toys and things to bring to children for Christmas.

I unpacked all the fishing gear, set up a rod and reel for Steven and the wife because they were getting anxious to fish. Especially after the trials and tribulation trying to get to this spot. I attached catfish rigs to both poles. These are a hook with some bait like corn on it and a heavy lead sinker put on the line. Then I threw it out as far out as I could—more towards the middle of the river where most catfish swim. Typically, catfish swim out in the middle of the river, where there's more current, which would mean more food passing by for them to catch.

I stood a couple of feet from the shoreline, casting my rig way out in the water. To my left was Steven, who was maybe 15 feet away. And to his left, maybe 20 feet or more down the shoreline, was Christina. And there we were, secluded, lines in the water and trying to catch fish. And I was in heaven!

We fished for about an hour to an hour and a half but to no avail. We tried different lures, different bait, and anything else that we could think of to catch fish. But it seemed we were not going to catch anything that day. I certainly didn't want my son disappointed and going home empty-handed. I would have been happy if he had caught a little minnow, but he was having fun just being with his dad.

I have fished this river for many years, and usually, there would always seem to be a strong current but not on this day. Plus, it was quiet, almost unnaturally so. There was no sound, no wind, just dead calm, and this didn't feel right. It felt weird.

I was standing there on the shore periodically looking at the oil refinery and pondering how they process oil to make gasoline and plastics when it happened; that weird feeling I sometimes get when someone is staring at me! That's a strange feeling to have, especially when you don't see another person anywhere.

I was looking all around us to see if anyone else was there. Who could be back here in this secluded place, I thought? Is someone hiding in the bushes behind us? Is someone staring at me from across the river? My mind was racing, and I was asking myself all types of questions. I thought this would be the perfect place for someone to do us harm. It was that secluded. It seemed we were all alone, but somehow we must not have been.

What I didn't understand at the time was the gift and how it worked. The gift gives me that strange feeling like someone is staring at me, but I was not aware of it nor its magnitude. Today I look forward to that feeling of being stared at, but I was mystified and even a little frightened of it back then. I know now that it's the beings on the UFOs that are the ones staring at me and not anyone else.

As I was standing on the shoreline fishing and having that feeling, I looked almost straight up. I don't know why I looked where I did because I could have looked anywhere, but instead, I cranked my head skyward. That's when I noticed a large flock of white birds. I believe they were seagulls. There were many birds in this flock, maybe 40 – 50. And they were all in a tight bunch, flying in, out, and around each other. It was almost hypnotic. I thought, could it be the birds that are giving me this all-consuming feeling?

What was so odd to me was the birds weren't making any sound. I thought seagulls would make a lot of noise because I know they screech and squawk, but these birds were utterly silent. In fact, I didn't hear any sound coming from anywhere. I felt like I was in a soundproof room. Were they silent, or were my ears blocked somehow? There was no wind, no waves, and it looked like there wasn't even a current in the river. Just dead calm, and that seemed very unnatural to me.

As I was still trying to resolve the fact that someone, somewhere, was still staring at me, it then hit me like a ton of bricks. I was quite surprised because above the flock of birds, maybe another 100 feet up or so, were two identical round, silver UFOs just hovering there. I don't know why I never noticed them above the flock of birds in the first place.

This is where we were fishing and the location of the UFO.

I guess I could call them the typical saucer-shaped UFO. They were considerably large, maybe 75 - 100 feet in diameter and 15 - 20 feet thick. Both UFOs were identical and dull metallic silver. There were no lights of any kind and no openings or cracks. Neither UFO had any windows or portholes. There were no markings on either UFO. And no indication of any combustion engine. I heard no sound or humming noise or any static charge as other UFO witnesses have commented.

When I see a craft, any craft, either hovering or flying, I always expect to hear some kind of noise. That's because our airplanes make a lot of engine noise, but these UFOs were otherworldly silent. They weren't wobbling or rocking as others have said, too—just two stunning and wondrous UFOs hovering above me. Now I was in heaven!

My mind was not expecting to see two UFOs, and at first, I was in some kind of daze, stunned actually. It was so baffling to me that I was even questioning my sanity. After finally grasping the situation, which took me probably 10 - 15 seconds to realize what I was looking at, I thought, wow, two beautiful UFOs, right there above my son and me. And seeing a UFO this time wasn't scary at all! On the contrary, I was in awe at what I was seeing. It had been so very long since that fateful night at the cabin. And this sighting was during the daytime too. Maybe that's why I wasn't scared. These weren't on fire, either, which in itself was terrifying. These were solid objects hovering above me, and I could just stand there and enjoy the show.

The orientation of one of these UFOs was quite extraordinary. You would expect things in the air like an airplane or helicopter to have their bottom located parallel with the earth, right? Planes fly horizontal and only change angles slightly upward on takeoff and downward when landing. This would be a reasonable assumption, but for some reason, one of the craft, the one on the right, was hovering vertically while the other UFO on the left was horizontal. The UFO on the right was hovering with its base towards the ship on the left. I noticed it had a small round top pointing right.

The left side UFO was hovering silently, too, but was oriented normally or horizontally. Because the left UFO orientation was horizontal, the ship's base is what I saw more of, and presume it had the same small rounded top just like the other UFO.

This is exactly what we witnessed over the Mississippi.

If they both had smaller round tops where I presume the occupants were sitting, that would mean they were, in fact, about 15-20 feet in depth. I saw no exhaust vents or vapor trails like our planes and cars have. I felt no static electricity, as some folks have claimed.

I thought that the UFO on the right was in a different kind of dimension or something because of its orientation. How or even why would a craft hover in the vertical position is beyond me. How could the occupants be comfortable and able to get up from what I presume would be a sitting position and walk around? They must have conquered gravity, and maybe that's why the one ship was vertical. I don't know, nor do I understand it even today. Of all the UFOs that I have witnessed over the years, this was the only ship to hover in a vertical position.

I didn't want to overt my eyes. I was going to stare at those UFOs for as long as I could and was hoping they would stay there hovering above me because I was enjoying the sighting so much.

As I stared at both of them for a couple of minutes or more, I thought, hey, wait a minute, I need a witness. As I was staring at them, I called over to my son, who was slightly down the beach. I was pointing up at the UFOs, and I yelled to him, hey, Steven, what are those things up there? Steven looked up and immediately replied, "Those are UFOs, Dad! Wow, my first UFO, how cool!" We both stood there on the shore and just stared at the two ships. Neither of us talked anymore. My rod and reel were down by my side, and I was staring up at this fantastic event. For me, it was surreal.

I am not sure how long Steven and I stood there, staring at those ships. Maybe a couple of minutes more. However long it was, it was long enough because my neck was getting sore from having it in an unnatural bend since I was the one looking at them the longest.

After a few minutes of being captivated by those ships, I stopped staring at them and looked over at Steven and said, pretty cool, huh?

He had a huge smile on his face and said, "Those are awesome, Dad!" I replied, I know, right?

Since I wasn't frightened at this event, it appeared neither was Steven. He seemed overwhelmed with joy! And since that day, it has profoundly changed my son. He has looked to the skies ever since. Sometimes I feel that his wanting to see another UFO borders on obsession. When we talk on the phone, the subject always turns to UFOs. He nearly always asked me if I've seen any more of them.

Then Steve and I looked down the shoreline at Christina. She was 20 feet or so away from Steven and still fishing. She never noticed the two UFOs at all. When we looked at Christina, we both shouted to her in unison as we were pointing up, hey Christina, look up there. There are 2 UFOs! Steven and I looked back at each other in utter amazement because we expressed the same words simultaneously and with the identical inflection as in a choir. Steven looked back at me, and we both laughed at what we just did. Christina didn't seem to hear us and kept fishing, so I shouted to her again while pointing upwards, Christina, look there, there's a couple of UFOs!

After I had called down to her that second time, then all three of us looked up. To our dismay, both UFOs had disappeared. She said, "What? You saw a what? A UFO?" Steven said, "Aw, they're gone, Dad!" With my head up, I said, doggonit, they're gone! Steven asked, "Where did they go, Dad? Did they just fly away or something? Could they still be there, and we just can't see 'em anymore?" I said, you mean, are they camouflaged? He said, "Oh yea, that thing." I told him, I just don't know, Steve. I don't know where they could have gone.

I am not sure if they both took off together or not. Or maybe the two UFOs cloaked themselves somehow to hide from our sight. Perhaps they controlled our minds to make it seem like they were not there anymore. Could they have just shot out of sight in just those few seconds, I thought? Not hearing any sound, I was thinking, possibly, but one thing was for sure, they were both gone, and the sighting was over! I was bummed out and exhilarated at the same time. This sighting was the longest one I have ever had. It was over five minutes long and just wonderful. And to have my son with me was so incredible too.

Neither Steve nor I knew what happened to them. All we knew was it bummed us both out. After the sighting was over, Steven asked all kinds of questions about UFOs and aliens and such. I tried to answer his questions as best I could, but I was in the same boat. I didn't know anything more about what was going on than he did. We kept fishing and talking for about another hour or so and then stopped. We packed everything up and went back through the gauntlet of sticker bushes again.

I was still in a kind of daze because of the sighting, and I forgot to look at my watch. I snapped out of it and checked the time to make sure no time had passed unexpectedly, which could mean an abduction scenario. But the time was as it should be, so no, we didn't get abducted. I'm happy we didn't get abducted and or experimented on by aliens.

I have read several books about others who have witnessed an event like this too. Aliens abducted the people, and while in the UFO, they were experimented on and then let go. Once freed, those people noticed that a significant amount of time had passed. I won't discuss the details of what kind of experiment the captors had performed on those poor people. I'll just say this isn't something I would care to happen to my son and wife or me, for that matter.

After we got home, the UFO subject was on our minds and in our conversations for months. Neither he nor I saw another one that year. Actually, this was the only sighting with Steven and me together. Although I've had a life with UFOs, Steve, on the other hand, has never seen an actual ship.

Since that fateful day on the Mississippi, I have always wondered about those two UFOs and why they happen to be where they were. Was this event just happenstance? Maybe? Maybe not. The UFO at Pipe Lake was before Steve was born, and I thought that perhaps these UFOs were there not only for me to witness them, but maybe they were checking out my son Steve and wife Christina. I did have the feeling before the actual sighting that someone somewhere was staring at me. And before the sighting I had an all-consuming feeling of needing to fish in this exact spot. At the time, I didn't realize just how that was going to weave itself ultimately and entirely into my life and the lives of my loved ones.

The beings on those ships could have been analyzing the oil refinery across the river, maybe to make diagrams or something. Perhaps they wanted to investigate how we process oil to produce gasoline and other by-products developed using oil.

I read about a UFO sighting that utilized lights on the bottom of the craft and was shining those lights onto the ground vegetation. It seemed to the people involved in the sighting that the UFO was observing the ground cover and were not interested in them. Are these visitors from another planet gathering information about our planet, and what do they want to know? Any UFO sighting can unnerve a person because no one wants to be involved in an abduction scenario. A sighting of a UFO is one thing, but abduction is quite another!

Coming up in the next chapter will be the gift happening again. I should have felt frightened to go to a convenience store on a bustling street during the day and see a UFO. But it felt like it was just an everyday occurrence that no matter where I lived or with whom, I was going to see more UFOs. This majestic daytime sighting made me finally realize that I am intertwined with beings from another planet and that I will enjoy a life with UFOs.

Again I had another witness with me during this sighting. Are they only here for me? Or do they want me to be with other people during the sightings? At the time, I didn't know which one it was, but that question would finally be answered and soon.

3

UFO Above 7-Eleven

"One theory which can no longer be taken very seriously is that UFOs are interstellar spaceships."
Arthur C. Clarke,
New York Times Book Review, 07/27/75.

In the last chapter, my UFO sighting happened in 1993. Several years before then, I had a car accident. While stopped at a traffic light, I was rear-ended by a young man racing through traffic and didn't see me. My brand new 1990 red T-top Chevy Camaro and I traveled through the intersection while I had both feet pushed down on the brake as hard as I could. My neck and back slammed and contorted into the seat, and I was severely injured. I tore ligaments and must have ripped cartilage because I was in a state of severe pain.

My neck got better after a few months, but my upper back between my shoulder blades didn't. My back was aching so much that I went to many different doctors and chiropractors for treatment with no relief. I would get this stabbing pain right behind my left shoulder blade at times of physical stress like mowing the lawn. Even walking caused me distress.

Each fall from 1990 through October 1995, my children and I would volunteer our time to the Walk for M.S. That's a 15-mile walk on a predetermined course for the Multiple Sclerosis Society. I would ask family and friends to donate any amount of money per mile of walking that they wished. I would walk as many miles as possible, up to the predetermined course length, which was 15 miles long. Most donated a dollar a mile, so if I made it to the end of the course, the person contributed $15.

When I first started walking, I would get this sharp pain behind my left shoulder blade in my back. That intense, stabbing pain would go away after a mile or so, and then everything would be fine.

Even though I saw lots of doctors, the pain persisted. It went on like this for over five years. I did worry that there could be something wrong with my heart, so I went to see a cardiologist. I had several treadmill stress tests to see if there was any blockage in my heart, but they found nothing.

A stress test is a way a cardiologist can check your heart for signs of obstruction. I would get on a treadmill, and they would increase the speed and angle of the tread stressing your heart. Running on a treadmill brought my heart bpm or beats per minute from a resting number of 70 bpm to 200 bpm. Some of you will not believe the 200 bpm, but I'm telling the truth. I saw that number when I was doing a stress test. Nowadays, doctors don't have to stress the heart that much. If I had a blocked artery in my heart, there would be changes in the electrical signals. The doctor put sensors all over my chest, connected to an EKG or electrocardiogram machine to see any changes.

My mother and I would talk about my aching back all the time. I told her that I would get this sharp pain and couldn't get any doctors to tell me what was causing it or why. I told her I was still in discomfort. Even though I had several stress tests, and they found nothing. I asked her what was I to do now? She insisted that I go back to the cardiologist and have them look more closely at my heart. As she said to me, that is the problem, Raymond. She was adamant about it and never let up.

So that's what I did. I went back to the hospital, where I had the test done, and saw a new cardiologist. He had looked at all the older stress tests and said, Mr. Groschen, let me assure you of one thing; there is nothing wrong with your heart! He asked me when was the last time I had a stress test performed? I informed him that it was just a few months ago right here at St. John's Hospital. He asked, what did your doctor tell you back then? I told him that I was switching cardiologists at that time, and I never received a phone call about the results. I said, anyway, you're my new cardiologist now. He said, OK, I will look up those results. As a side note, I had changed cardiologists, and this new doctor never got my latest stress test results.

He came back into the room about 10 minutes later and was looking completely white! I said to him, what is wrong with you? You look like you just saw a ghost or something! He told me he was going to check me into the hospital as soon as possible for further tests. I was shocked! I asked him what's wrong? He told me the last stress test showed that I had some severe trouble with my heart, and I needed further testing right away and is something I can't put off.

Now I was freaked out. My father died at 51 from a massive heart attack while doing his daily 3-mile walk to keep himself in shape. And I'm only 39, and I got severe heart trouble? I said, what do you mean by severe heart trouble? He said he couldn't elaborate more than that, and I'll have to wait for more sophisticated testing, which will give me more accurate results.

I asked the doctor exactly what kind of more sophisticated tests are they going to perform? He told me the hospital would do an angiogram. He explained that an angiogram is a diagnostic test that uses x-rays to take pictures of my heart blood vessels. A long flexible catheter will be inserted into a vein near my groin area through the bloodstream up to the heart to deliver a dye or contrast agent where the arteries will become more visible on the x-ray. This test will show us if and where there is any blockage, he said.

He suggested I go back home and NOT do any kind of stressful activity like mowing the lawn or anything like that. He told me everything would be OK and not to worry. Not to worry, I was beyond that by then. I was freaking out! I knew I had to settle down and just pray on it. Pray, everything will be alright, and I'm finally in good hands now.

How could there be something that serious with my heart? I was in good shape. Not great, but I did things for myself that I thought was going to save me from my genetics. After dad passed away, I decided that I wasn't going to end up like him. I took an aspirin every day to thin my blood, making it more difficult to create heart blockages. I stopped smoking. I exercised by walking all over St. Paul, Minnesota, with the kids. I walked every year for the M.S. Society, going 15 miles every time. I played softball and golfed more times than I could count. When I would golf, I never road in a cart to exercise my heart, trying to keep it in good shape. And I ate well or as best as I could to keep my weight down. So why on God's green earth would I have something wrong with my heart?

I'm going to share something with you that some of you won't believe. You CANNOT run from your family history, your genetics, and DNA. Take James FIXX in 1984. James F. Fixx, who spurred the jogging craze with his best-selling books about running and preached the gospel that active people live longer, died of a massive heart attack while on a jog in Vermont. He was 52 years old.

Mr. Fixx, the author of five books, among them "The Complete Book of Running," was found dead at 5:30 P.M. Mr. Fixx was genetically predisposed - his father died of a heart attack at 43 after a previous one at 35. What happens to your family can happen to you, so please heed my warning and beware.

I finally made it to the end of the week, and boy was that a long wait. I went to get the angiogram test done and find out just what this serious trouble was with my heart. As I was lying on the table during the test, I saw the doctor looking at a live feed of my heart on a T.V. screen. I could see my beating heart and all the veins too. He announced that they found three nearly 100% blocked arteries and that I'll have to have triple heart bypass surgery. He also told me that one of the blocked arteries was on the backside of my heart. Well, I'll be a monkey's uncle. Mom was right all along, and that's precisely why my back hurt for those years.

So, on October 10th, 1995, at the tender age of 39, I had a triple heart bypass surgery. As of this writing, it has been over 25 years with no other troubles. I don't even take high blood pressure medicine. Thank the dear Lord, and thank you, mom, for making me go in and get rechecked! If it wasn't for my mother demanding I go back and get another opinion, who knows, I might have ended up like poor Mr. Fixx or my dad for that matter.

After the surgery was over, I was lying in the hospital bed watching the news on the television. A reporter was interviewing a gentleman about the job he did and the amount of money he made. It seemed to the reporter that he made a hoard of money for what he was doing. To which he responded, the money doesn't matter. I love this job so much so that I would do it for free.

That statement struck me like a ton of bricks. This hit me so hard because I was in a job I hated, and the stress was enormous. I couldn't sleep. I drank way too much to try and help me sleep. Basically, I was a mess, and I needed to do something fast, or I could end up dad!

From 1983 until 1996, I was selling heating and air conditioning to homeowners and home builders or what we refer to as general contractors. We use the acronym HVAC, which stands for Heating, Ventilating & Air Conditioning.

In the middle of my selling HVAC, from 1987 until 1989, I owned my own company working with general contractors and homeowners. Selling to home builders was by far the highest stressful job I have ever had. I thought that most of the general contractors I did business with were criminals. And I especially hated dealing with them because they were always late on paying me.

Everything was going great with the business. After one year, we made over $20K. And that was after paying off all of our overhead like rent, wages, gas, and such. This is unheard of with a new company, and I knew it. There was just one more thing I had to do to really get us in the black.

We had to collect the outstanding balances from two contractors that were hesitating payment. They owed us $42K, and we needed that money to buy more air conditioners. On the same day, both issued us notice that they were filing no asset bankruptcies, and our $42,000 was gone. No asset bankruptcy means they wouldn't have anything for me to take and sell to get my money back. Nor did they have any assets like a house I could have put a lien on to get my money back either.

Unfortunately, that was the straw that broke the camel's back per se', and I had to close up shop. As the owner, I then had to file personal as well as corporate no asset bankruptcies too.

Because of that, I had to go back to selling HVAC for another company, which was a very stressful time for me. I became a salesman for Vogt Heating and Cooling, one of the oldest and most well-respected HVAC companies in the Twin Cities. I brought along several of my well-paying high-profit home builders to Vogt. Those contractors were the best I had. I didn't want to lose them, especially since they always paid me on time. Bringing them over to this new company meant my sales could be somewhat respectable. And I was picking up new general contractors all the time.

Back then, most heating and air conditioning salespeople sold somewhere around $250-$400 thousand dollars annually. Mine started around that amount and was getting larger with each passing month. After one year, I was their top salesman.

I'm a goal-oriented person, so I grabbed a piece of paper and scribbled down a figure that I wanted to achieve for my annual sales amount. I put down $1,000,000.00. All the other salesmen thought I was nuts and told me so. They would continually make jokes about my goals because no one has ever had sales of over $500K annually as a residential salesman.

There were two types of salesmen back then. Commercial and residential. As the name implies, a commercial salesperson deals with commercial businesses like skyscrapers, factories, malls, and other commercial places. Obviously, there are many more air conditioners in a 50-story building than there is in one little home. It's a lot easier selling $1 million worth of HVAC equipment annually in commercial sales than in residential.

But I was firm in my conviction that I'll make that amount, and I told them in no uncertain terms. And after one year of selling for this new HVAC company, my sales amount was $1,000,025.00. I squeaked by and made my goal by $25. To say they were stunned is an understatement. The next thing I noticed on every salesmen's wall was a goal amount. I had to laugh. That was so funny to me, and I told them so. The year after that, I made $1.25 million, then up and up. In my fifth year selling for Vogt, I sold nearly two million dollars!

But through it all, it was so very stressful. I couldn't sleep more than four hours a night. I drank way too much, trying to help me sleep and being so stressed out that I could only put in about 4 hours of work a day, which I hid from them. They all thought I was working overtime to reach the limits I had achieved. I hated what I was doing. I absolutely hated every single minute of selling to home builders. I needed a way out of this predicament, or the job was going to kill me, I thought.

I also found out something interesting about the two builders that stiffed me for the $42,000. Unbeknownst to me, just a year before doing business with them, they were identified as a different company name and had filed no asset bankruptcies. They stiffed a lot of other subcontractors just like they stiffed me. Then they reopened under a new name and started withholding monies from other subcontractors precisely as they did to me. I would have thought doing things like this would be a crime like fraud, but it was legal. It was completely unethical, but that was how contractors did things in those days in Minnesota. They could start a business, take money from unsuspecting subcontractors, and go out of any business. And do this over and over again with no ramifications!

Finding out that information about those contractors was a revelation because I acquired this information on the internet. And it was reasonably straightforward. I just queried the contractor's name and found some fascinating information on them.

The internet at that time was not the internet you know today. English scientist Tim Berners-Lee invented the world wide web or the WWW in 1991, a few years before I was able to find the information. So, getting that was pretty cool.

I thought about the implications of getting this information to other subcontractors like me and how it could help them not fall in with a bad general contractor. I decided to open a business website to get that info to all subcontractors.

I needed a name for the site that a subcontractor could relate to, so they would know I was there to help. I would be promoting this information only to sub-contractors. I decided to call it Sub-ContractorsCreditReportingService.com. I know it's a cumbersome name, but that was then, and that's how we did things to get higher ratings in the search engines. Back then, the keywords people would use to search for a company had to be in the website name.

I knew this information would be precious to other subs like me because it would protect their business. That's because they could be working for a crooked general contractor, and my information would show them precisely that.

I knew that this concept was a goldmine because, in 1990, there was no one anywhere in the world that supplied information about home builders to subcontractors. I found liens, judgments, bankruptcies, and, most of all, name changes. I could now follow the company owner, not just the company name but the name of the people who owned it. In the database I created, the subcontractor could see a chronological series of negative information on a home builder. The general contractor could not hide under the name of the company anymore. I sold monthly subscriptions to all types of subcontractors. They could now check on any builder they wanted to work with, even the ones they were already working with, which helped them collect any outstanding debts. And before the general contractor filed a no-asset bankruptcy, as they did to me. Pretty cool, huh?

In 1993 there were no AngiesList.com or HomeAdvisors.com. I was the very first company to offer this on the internet. It could have gone national, and I recognized that. On a side note, I changed that long name to one more fitting; ContractorFacts.com.

I acquired many subcontractors who were buying the information. I could have easily kept up with ContractorFacts.com and made it a national company, but I was in a quandary about all of this. Do I genuinely want to keep promoting this information or keep selling heating and air conditioning equipment or both? I decided to slow down selling that information to subcontractors and sold off ContractorFacts.com some years later, which gave me time to compose this book.

I know what you're thinking. Dude, you had a billion-dollar idea. Money should never enter into the equation. If you don't follow a happy, joyful, and stress-free life, you could end up with more significant troubles than a triple bypass. Stress can bring things like cancer, high blood pressure causing strokes, and other ailments. Stress will make physiological changes in your body, so it's best to do what you can to relieve it. I can attest to that.

To me, no amount of money will ever make me truly happy. I have to be spiritually happy, not monetarily happy. Who knew stress could do that to the body.

I knew in my heart (nice pun) what the problem was. The stress from dealing with general contractors in any form represented my dilemma and the key reason I needed bypass surgery. The way out of that enormous stress was to get retrained for a different job. And one I would love and would not care if I got paid or not. Just like the person in that T.V. interview. To me, that was another revelation. You would think that this would be conventional wisdom, but a lot of people right now are stuck working at a place they hate and can't or don't do anything about it.

After hearing the reporter interviewing that gentleman about his job made me think. That idea just kept swirling around and around in my head. I could hardly think of anything else. I thought about that continually after I initially heard that man answer that question.

Months went by, and I kept asking myself what I could do where I would love a job that much? After much contemplation, two things came to mind: 1) being a surgical nurse, which I've always dreamed about, and 2) since I was working on the internet, I thought that somehow I could achieve a career there. But I did not know what job positions there were or how to be retrained in them.

Then I looked on the internet at different positions back then regarding what people do when working on the internet. There were positions like software programming, computer technician, webmaster, and a few more.

I found more information on what a webmaster was and found that a webmaster is a person who develops websites, all kinds of websites like e-commerce sites. Amazon, Nabisco, or anyone who wants to promote their wares on the internet had to secure a webmaster to design the website. Back then, webmasters did all the images and all the back-end coding, which was just what I was looking to do, especially for a person who gets easily bored. A webmaster was also responsible for writing the worldwide content of the companies they're working for, and I did love to write.

That sounded refreshing because I already made a website, created a database of information, and started a search form so subcontractors could search their general contractors all by themselves. I read as much as I could to find out about being a webmaster, which then became my second choice for a new and exciting career.

I left it up to God and flipped a coin. Heads I would go to surgical nursing college, and tails I would be a webmaster. So, I flipped the coin, and it came up tails – webmaster would be my new career, but where do I go to school for this?

I looked on the internet for a school that would allow me to work as a webmaster. In 1995 there were not many Universities that offered that specific job title, but I finally found one that did. I found it at The University of Advancing Computer Technologies in Tempe, Arizona, a Phoenix suburb.

At the start of 1996, I gave my 2-week notice, moved my wife and I and all our belongings down to Phoenix, AZ. We moved into Bell Lakes Apartments on 33rd avenue and Bell Road in Glendale, AZ, another Phoenix suburb. I arrived in Phoenix on April 28th, 1996, and proceeded to move all my things in.

One of the first things I did after I moved into my new apartment was to check out the school. The school was located in Tempe, which was a short drive from the apartment. Their curriculum was exactly what I was looking for and allowed me to retrain as a webmaster. I was in heaven. No more stress, no more sleepless nights, and no more bypass surgeries. Truly outstanding! I signed on the dotted line and started school that fall. After a couple of years of school, I graduated being on the dean's list every semester and culminating with top honors. I received an A.A. degree in Multimedia/Computer Science.

I was now a webmaster on the internet, and I loved that job. I enjoyed it so much I genuinely didn't care if I got paid or not. And yes, I did a few websites for free and didn't mind if I got paid. You see, you can change careers and love what you're doing too. I created over 700 websites as a webmaster and loved every minute of it! And, I made between $60,000 - $105,000 a year playing on the internet. Who wouldn't love that?

I gave this short history because on June 12th, 1997, at noon just over a year after coming down to Phoenix, I was at the apartment studying for a big test coming up. I got this feeling like I needed to leave right then. I thought I needed more cigarettes, but the pack was half full, and I had another one in the frig. What was giving me this feeling, I thought. Something was urging me, literally pulling me out of the apartment, and for what? A pack of smokes? It reminded me of what happened on the Mississippi. That same intense feeling of needing to go fishing, even though I didn't want to go. Just like then, an all-consuming feeling but from where or from who?

I gave in to the feeling and got up, walked out of my apartment, and headed for the closest convenience store. One block away was a 7-Eleven. I bought some smokes and headed out the door to light one up. As I was standing in front of the 7-Eleven, something extraordinary happened.

After a couple of minutes of puffing on the cigarette, the gift happened and reared its fantastic head. I had that strange feeling like someone somewhere was staring at me again. I did what I did before. I looked up, but this time I did not look overhead as I did on the Mississippi; I looked up just above the 7-Eleven. And much to my surprise, there it was, a dull metallic silver, bell topped UFO. As if my mind's eye knew precisely where this UFO was hovering.

I knew then that I must have a gift, but who gave it to me? And why was I chosen to witness so many beautiful UFOs? I'm no one special, just an ordinary guy who loves seeing UFOs. Are they trying to communicate with me somehow? Do others on earth have this gift too? And what's so very strange to me is I have more sightings with witnesses than by being alone. Are they trying to introduce themselves to our world? I think that is the answer. They're showing themselves more today than ever before and to more people. I'm still asking these questions and wondering why me, though.

I would call the Minnesota UFOs the typical silver saucer-shaped type and a multiple person craft. But this one was a lot smaller in diameter, maybe 10 - 15 feet wide and only about 8 feet high. And it had a pronounced bell-shaped top. I believe it could have been the same color as the two UFOs in Minnesota, but I'm not exactly sure. It was pretty close to that dull metallic silver color if it wasn't.

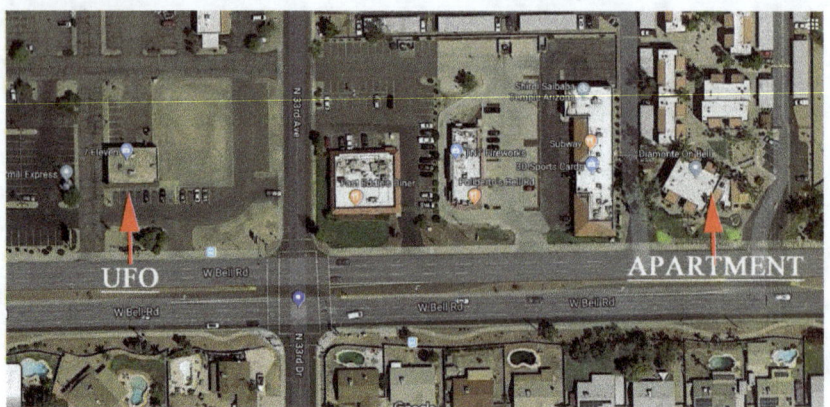

Here's the location of the UFO sighting.

Given my previous experiences with UFOs, I knew not to move, not to avert my eyes. And if someone would happen to walk by, I would still stare at the UFO and just tell the person to look up. I was not going to allow this baby to disappear, no way, Jose.

Right then, a guy did come walking down the same sidewalk and came near me. I said while staring at the UFO, Dude, look up, what do you see? He said, "Oh my GOD! It's a freaking UFO!" He didn't say the word freaking but you get the point. I said, I know, I've been standing here staring at it for a couple of minutes now, and I don't want to look away. I know if I look away, it'll disappear. We both stood there in awe. Wow, another UFO, right around noon, hovering 100 feet above a 7-Eleven in Glendale, AZ, and on a very busy street. Plus, I had another witness too.

Neither of us was anxious nor afraid. We were both in shock. I thought this UFO was spectacular, and unusual, and so very cool, and was overjoyed. I have not been frightened of UFOs since that first sighting on Pipe Lake. On the contrary, I love seeing them. These UFOs have not made any threatening or harassing movements towards me. Nor have I experienced any missing time as in an abduction scenario. So, I don't have to worry when a UFO sighting happens. I can have a UFO sighting without fear and enjoy it.

With me, most sightings are longer than a few seconds, and so far, they've stayed for many minutes. I can start to take mental notes on the UFOs' characterization, especially for UFO reporting services such as the National UFO Reporting Center or nuforc.org. That's if I make an online report.

The craft was a lot smaller than the two UFOs on the Mississippi. Most likely a single occupant craft, but who knows? I couldn't believe the UFO could hold more than one occupant because it was that small. The other thing was the strength of the staring part was less too. It seemed the two UFOs on the Mississippi had many beings on them, and all of them were staring at me at once. But with this small UFO, it felt like there was only one being staring at me.

What I do remember was there were no sound and no humming. It was so near to us that I could see it had no windows, no openings or cracks. There were no identifying marks. I saw no lights on this craft, either. Just one beautiful dull metallic silver UFO with a bell-shaped top above us, and it was spectacular!

He and I stood there for a couple of minutes more. Then I did something I regret to this day, I looked over at him and said, Oh, by the way, my name is Ray. He shook my hand and told me, "Hi, I'm Bill", and he just came to the 7-Eleven to get some bread or something. I forget what he said to me exactly. The street was so busy and noisy during the sighting that Bill and I were nearly shouting at each other just to make out what each of us was saying.

RAY GROSCHEN

This is exactly what Bill and I witnessed.

A close-up look at the bell-shaped UFO Bill and I witnessed.

After our short conversation, we both looked back up at the UFO, and it was gone. The same thing happened as the other two craft on the Mississippi. He looked at me and said, "Dude, where did it go? Oh well, that was pretty cool!" I merely shrugged my shoulders and shook my head, but in my mind, I was more like, DAMN IT, DAMN IT, DAMN IT! I should not have looked elsewhere. I know they can travel fast, but that would have been super fast. I think that they can maybe cloak themselves too. Who knows. Naturally, all of this is speculation. I am not sure what happened to the craft. It just disappeared.

Believe it or not, I never got Bill's phone number, so I can't precisely relay what he experienced about the sighting. I am relating what he stated as best as I could remember. I do know he was quite amazed and ecstatic at this UFO sighting.

Oh, how I wished I possessed something to take a picture of this UFO. Remember, this was way before cell phones and phone cameras. There was just no way to lug around a camera unless I knew they were coming. If it happened more rapidly, say faster than every four or five years, and were a once a month thing, well then heck yea, I would have all sorts of image taking stuff with me to capture a picture of a UFO. But back then, no way, man.

I wonder why nobody else noticed this UFO. Since that time, I have repeatedly checked all UFO reporting websites to see if anyone else witnessed this bell-shaped UFO. As far as I can tell, we were the only ones who saw it. It's so hard for me to believe because the sighting was smack dab in the middle of the day. It was lunchtime, and there's a lot of businesses and employees around at that time getting lunch. There are more apartment buildings around that 7-Eleven than I can count, yet no one saw the UFO? Plus, that particular convenience store is on Bell road, a 6-lane thoroughfare that travels for dozens of miles through many cities. It's a boisterous, bustling street. It's one of the main streets through Glendale and one of Phoenix's busiest. Yet we were the only witnesses? How truly odd.

After the UFO disappeared, Bill and I said our goodbyes. We didn't say any more than that because I think we were both still in shock. I sauntered back to my apartment, reflecting on the sighting and wondering what if anything will happen in the future. I remembered that I had to get my school work done, so I stepped up my pace. I had to finish studying for a mid-term test later that day and had to keep my grade point average at 4.0 and stay on the dean's list, which I accomplished.

I checked the clock when I got back to the apartment. Wondering if there was any missing time, but no, everything was as it should be. Thank God that neither Bill nor I were abducted. I guess we were there just to see the UFO.

Plus, I have to tell you, it's tough trying to study for a test after having a UFO sighting like that, and I can attest to that! My thoughts kept going back to the sighting, and I was having trouble concentrating on my schoolwork.

The UFO was gone, and I was upset, but on the other hand, I was ecstatic, too, because this was my 3rd sighting. Without a doubt, the gift was working again with this sighting. At the time, I started to understand more about this gift and thought about how lucky I was to witness so many extraordinary kinds of ships in numerous states. The count is four UFOs in three separate states. Most people never have one UFO encounter, but I've had multiple contacts in different parts of the country, so what is going on?

Was it just luck, or was all this a ruse? I thought that maybe they want me as an ambassador of some sort. I don't know, but whatever the reasons, UFOs made themselves visible to me, and most of the time, I'm with other people.

I reflected on all my UFO sightings that I've had up to that point. And that I had that strange feeling of being stared at again but from who? I was wondering why me? Am I really that special? I knew that someone somewhere chose me for this responsibility, and I'm more than grateful for it. But was Bill chosen too, or was it just dumb luck that he happened to walk to that particular store at that precise moment.

Sitting at my kitchen table, I thought about my life journey and the things I've chosen to do, and the places where I thought I decided to live. In our life journeys, are we first put in a boat to aimlessly float down a river, and we cannot go back upstream, switch streams, or even go back to the shoreline? Or do we sit in the boat and row in any direction we feel is right for us? Are we in control of our lives, or does a higher power, a higher self, if you will manage everything we do? I know I'm getting a little philosophical here, but that's only because I was in a quandary about what was going on back then with all the UFOs I was being presented with.

I've come to an understanding that it's probably both. We have some control and not. I believe we're born with a predetermined life plan that can change, given the circumstances. Meaning this; the life plan we come to earth with is predestined to learn spiritual lessons. We are brought to these lessons each and every day. If we don't learn from our mistakes, we are redirected to the same lesson again. But in a different manner, until we finally get it. If not, you'll be presented with that lesson over and over again.

If it weren't for the triple heart bypass and me wanting to switch careers, I would not have come down to Phoenix. Since I have been here, I have witnessed so many unusual things it has blown my mind. What I mean by unusual, I mean, as in 17 more UFO sightings! If I didn't need bypass surgery, would I have seen as many UFOs in Minnesota as I've witnessed down in Phoenix? I sincerely doubt that but who really knows for sure? What I do know is that the gift is strong here!

Going from owning a house in St. Paul, Minnesota, to living in an apartment in Phoenix, Arizona, wasn't all that great. We were getting tired of apartment living because you dump vast amounts of money into something that gives you no return. We wanted to get back to owning another house for our future financial stability. But for now, I had to concentrate on my schoolwork to achieve my ultimate goal. Starting a job that I would love so much that I wouldn't care if I got paid or not.

The last two sightings were the gift working because of that strange stared at the feeling I had, but who was doing the staring? And were those previous two UFO sightings predetermined or dumb luck? I was certain at that point that I'd been chosen for something greater than myself but wasn't sure what that something might be. Will I witness more UFO's, or is this it, I thought? I guess one can't know for sure, but the gift was going to rear its magnificent head in just a few more years. The following chapter will be a real doozy of a sighting and something that is definitely NOT of this earth!

4

UFO over Grand Avenue

> "The phenomenon of UFOs is real. I know that there are scientific organizations which study the problem."
> Former Soviet President Mikhail Gorbachev,
> 26th April 1990.

It is now the summer of 1998, and our lease was up at the apartment. Christina and I didn't want to rent anymore. Since we sold our house in St. Paul, Minnesota, we wanted to get back into a home rather than rent. We looked for a place down here but couldn't afford one back then. We looked everywhere and talked to banks and realtors galore but no luck.

One realtor, however, suggested that we look at a manufactured house to purchase. We looked at many different sizes and styles and finally found a new double-wide mobile home that we thought would be a good substitute. At first, I was hesitant to purchase a mobile home or trailer because of the stigma of owning one. Up in Minnesota, people who own one are quietly referred to as trailer trash since many live near or below the poverty line. But after seeing several units, I was convinced these were an excellent replacement. And more than reasonable to afford at only $52K.

There are two types of mobile homes, a single wide and a double-wide. The main difference between them is the amount of floor space. Generally, single-wide mobile homes are available between 600 and 1,330 square feet. All single-wide mobile homes must be 18 feet wide or less and must be no longer than 90 feet. The most common dimensions for a single-wide are 15 feet wide by 72 feet long. Double-wide homes are much larger, typically measuring 26 feet wide by 56 feet long. Our double-wide home was more significant at 26 x 64 or 1664 square feet. It wasn't the biggest manufactured home since some can get to almost 2800 square feet, but it was certainly large enough for us.

The home came with four bedrooms and two baths with a large living room and a nice TV room. We purchased the mobile home and placed it at Orange Grove Estates on 67th avenue between Dunlap and Northern Avenues. Very close to the busy intersection 67th Avenue, Northern Avenue, and Grand Avenue interchange, which will become relevant in a little bit.

In 1999 and only being in the home for 1 1/2 years, our marriage wasn't doing well, not well at all. Christina was over ten years my junior and never quite got out of the partying and drinking modes. She would come creeping in a 5 am on many occasions. She was treading water and the second marriage was on the rocks. Actually, it was drowning. Finally, having had enough, I told her I wanted a divorce.

Once we finalized the divorce, I was happy again being on my own and started dating once more. I wanted to party hardy and date other women and have some fun without all the bickering. I would go to the local R & B club, Club Central, for some dancing. I found a few guy friends, which I hadn't had in decades, and we met up every Friday night at Club Central. It was a lot of fun, which I hadn't had in a long, long time.

You could meet a lot of people at Club Central. I met a Southwest Airlines flight attendant and offered to take her out to dinner.

She was from a different part of the country and was laying over in Phoenix for one night. After finishing our date, she asked me if it would be OK if she gave my cell number to other flight attendants lying over in Phoenix and looking for a fun time. I told her that it would be a great idea.

The next week I had a date every night from Monday to Friday, and loving it. That went on for a few months. Most of these women were half my age and just looking to have some fun, and I was more than willing to accommodate. Believe it or not, I was getting exhausted and wanted to pull back on the reigns as it were, so I stopped dating the flight attendants and concentrated on just a couple of local women I knew. It was fun while it lasted, but I'm not really that kind of guy.

I was looking to slow things down a bit and met a couple of women at Club Central and started dating them. One I met was a lovely woman named Kelsey. Like the flight attendants, she was only 28 years old, and I was 43! A lot younger than me but mature for her age. Even though the relationship came with three kids, I didn't mind because I love kids. I'm sorry, I don't remember the children's names, but I do remember how old they were at the time. Kelsey's oldest was a girl at 13. She had another girl who was six and a son that was five years old. We all enjoyed doing things together. Kelsey wasn't ready for marriage, and neither was I. Actually, I never ever wanted to be married again! Two marriages were enough for me, especially the last marriage, which turned into a train wreck.

One day in the heat of the summer here, I called Kelsey to see if I could pick her and the children up and have them come over and take a dip in the community pool. Phoenix can get so hot in the summer that you can indeed fry an egg on the sidewalk. I've done it. This was precisely one of those days. Kelsey said that a dip in the pool sounds great. Since Kelsey didn't have a car, I got in mine and went over to her house. All four of them piled into the vehicle anticipating a nice refreshing swim. Especially the kids. They all had broad smiles on their faces and were so very happy. Almost the minute we got to my house, I remember the oldest girl saying, "Can we go to the pool now, mom, can we?" Kelsey said, "Sure, let's go."

The pool was about 100 yards or so from the house and a leisurely walk for Kelsey and her kids. Well, that's not entirely correct. We had to run to every shaded spot on the sidewalk we could find. We were getting from one shady place to the next until we got to the pool.

We were in the pool for about 30 minutes or so when her son said, "Hey Ray, what's that?" He pointed south towards my house at about a 45-degree angle from the ground. All of us looked over at what he was pointing at but were not sure what it was. It looked like it was the shape of a ball or something round, but that was all I could make out at that distance.

I thought maybe it was another UFO because as we sat in the pool looking at it for a couple of minutes, it moved a little to the left, and then it would slowly move back to the right, to its original position. We still had no idea what could be hovering there. I didn't get too excited because I didn't have that feeling of being stared at like those other UFO sightings, but I was undoubtedly getting curious. My curiosity was getting peaked, and I had to know what this thing was.

I asked Kelsey and the kids, hey, you guys want to go to the house and see it up close? I have a telescope we can look through. The youngest boy said, "Yea, mom, can we go see, can we?" Kelsey agreed, and we all got out of the pool, dried off in a hurry, and made our way as fast as we could to my house. I didn't want this object to disappear as all the others had, so we were running as quickly as our little feet could take us back to the house. We made it to the mobile home in a couple of minutes, dodging the sun-soaked ground again, going from one shade tree to the next, finally reaching my house.

When we got back to my house, I ran inside, grabbed my homemade red six-inch telescope, and ran outside as fast as possible, trying not to stumble or trip and break the scope. I wanted to know what it was and not disappear before getting the telescope set up to get a better look at it. I set the telescope up on the opposite side of the street, which gave me an excellent angle to view the object, and I could not believe my eyes.

It was a ball of flames! I said to myself, OMG, this is astounding. I witnessed one before but haven't seen anything like this so close up and personal before. The sighting at Pipe Lake, Wisconsin, was also a fireball, but that object was farther away and at night. And very hard to tell if they were the same type of fireball UFO. And we were so freaked out in that little boat that I couldn't determine exactly what it was. All we knew was it was somewhat bright, orange, and red and ball shaped, and on fire. And we were desperately trying to get away from whatever that was. This object, on the other hand, WAS a fireball UFO and huge at that. It had to be at least 40 - 50 feet in diameter!

I was thinking, why is there some strange object over by my house? This UFO or whatever it turns out to be could have been anywhere. Am I so entwined with them that they do what they can to make it easier for me to view them? Out of all the places to be on this earth, this was the only place where I would have had the greatest chance of seeing it so close up and personal.

I shouted to Kelsey, NO WAY! Kelsey said, "Why, what is it, Ray?" I said, Oh my God, Kelsey, it's a ball of fire! "No way!" she and the kids said almost in unison. I was beside myself; I couldn't believe what I was seeing. How could it be a perfectly round ball of fire hovering? And this time, it was during the day. Was I see this correctly? Has my mind started playing tricks on me?

I was seeing flames coming out all around it but not too far out. It's as if you went to the Sun and shrunk it to 50 feet in diameter. The flames were utterly symmetrical around the ball. Small yellow, orange, and red flames were jutting out just a couple of feet around this object.

Do you remember how the two UFOs on the Mississippi River were oriented? And how I said the UFO on the right seemed to be in a different dimension or something? Well, this ball of flames was similar to that. There was something very odd going on with this UFO.

The flames, which you would think would all be going up because flames are lighter than air, were, in fact, coming out from all around this thing and not turning upward. I will give you an example of what was happening with this ball of flames UFO; If you were to grab a lighter, and lite it, the flames are always pointing up, right? Now if you hold the cigarette lighter towards the ground and lite it again, what happens? Naturally, the flames would automatically turn upwards and you would burn your fingers, right? What would you think if the flames stayed pointing down to the ground? That's what was happening with this object.

On the bottom of this fireball, the flames were pointing to the ground and not turning up. This was the case with all the flames around this object. They were pointing outward and NOT at all turning up. This is an impossible scenario on earth. Flames do not work like that. The only thing I knew for sure was this couldn't be from our planet, and it had to be a UFO from somewhere else.

How could this be like that, I thought. Was this UFO in another dimension and not playing by the rules we have on earth. On this planet, we are governed by the law of gravity. Everything everywhere on earth, and for that matter, the entire universe conforms to the law of gravity. There are no exceptions to this rule. But this UFO was playing by its own rules somehow like it was inside a bubble where there were no consequences of gravity. And I was watching it do this odd behavior and was stunned.

The object was south of my home at 6707 West Northern Avenue. Near to the very busy interchange of Grand Avenue, W. Northern Avenue, and N. 67th Avenues. And here's the unbelievable thing about its location. Butting up to the wall in my backyard, south of my home, is ZyTech building systems, a lumber company. They manufacture wood roof trusses and other wood products used in homes! The ball of flames UFO was directly over them. Unfortunately, this sighting was on a Saturday, so no one was at ZyTech to witness it, just us.

The red star is the fireball UFO location, and the red arrow is my mobile home.

The youngest child shouted, "Let me see. Let me see!" I grabbed him around the waist and held him up to the eyepiece of the telescope. He said, "AW, cool mom!" but then said, "Ray, it's gone!" At first, I couldn't believe what he was saying. Did the UFO disappear as all those others had? It's gone, I shouted? Then I looked up, saw it, and pointed to it and said, No, look right there. There it is. I put the little boy down and peered back into the eyepiece. I couldn't see it, so I pulled my head away from the eyepiece of the telescope. Then I gazed up in the air where the UFO was, and the object had moved somehow to the left. I grabbed onto the top of the telescope tube. I panned the scope over to the left until I could see it in the eyepiece again. The UFO went about 100 feet or so to the left.

As I was staring at the object, something marvelous happened. The UFO slid over to the right, back to the exact spot where we had first observed it—maybe taking 2 - 3 seconds to perform. Looking through the telescope again, once more, the ball of flames started to shake. Just as if you held a basketball in your hands and shook it. This thing started shaking, and then zip it took off to the left. This was the UFOs routine. Nothing more, nothing less. We were watching this acrobatic routine, and knowing that it would perform it again and again. We watched the ball of flames do that acrobatic stunt for over 45 minutes.

I never heard any engine noise or humming or any static charge. I didn't see any windows or cracks—just one beautiful round ball of fire. And, of course, there weren't any markings on it either. The UFO never made any threatening moves towards us. It didn't land, and out comes some type of aliens from the Sun or something.

None of the children were worried or frightened. And above all, their mom Kelsey wasn't concerned for them either. She and the kids were all having a good time watching this ball of flames UFO as each child switched to view this UFO through the telescope. Everyone asked me why was it shaking and zipping to the left and sliding back? And why is it doing nothing else?

I have never figured out why the hovering, shaking and then zipping. And for as long as the UFO did these acrobatics. Nor could I figure out why it wouldn't conform to the law of gravity either. Through all these years, I have been checking the UFO reporting sites, and as far as I can tell, no one else was a witness to this sighting. All I knew was the gift worked wonderfully!

As with all the other UFO sightings, I knew I didn't want to avert my eyes. I just wanted to keep staring at the object so that it wouldn't disappear. This might sound strange, but we were all getting bored watching this fireball doing its acrobatics for over 45 minutes and just hovering 150 feet in the air, shaking and zipping.

Although it was over or very close to a bustling intersection, this was on a Saturday, so you would think that there would be tons of people driving past us, possibly being a witness to this sighting. I just can't believe that someone else didn't see this UFO. It was so big and so close to a bustling intersection! How could anyone not see a ball of flames 40 - 50 feet in diameter?

And the extremely unusual part about this was where my mobile home was located in conjunction with the fireball UFO. There are over a hundred mobile homes around me and hundreds of apartments within 100 - 200 yards of me. One must realize that this 3-way intersection is one of the busiest in all of Phoenix, too! I have never read that someone else witnessed this colossal fireball and am hoping someone will come forward. Maybe after reading this book.

I didn't know what to think or what this was, and my mind was looking for answers. Yea, it was a ball of flames, but from where? Why wasn't the fire going up like normal earthly flames do? Was there someone inside this fiery UFO like a flame being from the Sun or something? Was the UFO trying to start up, so they could leave? And go to where? What was truly going on, I wondered?

Now comes the regrettable part, at least for me about this remarkable sighting, Kelsey told me that it was time for her and the kids to get back home. Oh my God, I thought, I will miss something so extraordinary and phenomenal by having to leave. I begged her to stay. I said, Please, please, Kelsey, we need to keep watching this to know what will happen with it. This could be a once in a lifetime opportunity. Who knows, maybe we should alert someone to this new extremely sensational discovery! She said she knew how disappointed I was and that she wished her and the kids could remain. She apologized as best she could, but they had to get home. Her mother was coming back from vacation.

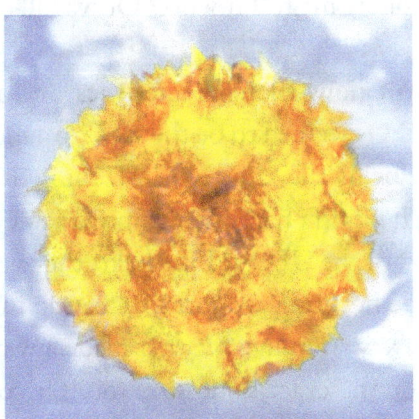

This was the fireball UFO we witnessed.

Here it was, a massive ball of flames UFO hovering near a very busy 3-way intersection in Glendale, Arizona, and being in the middle of the day doing some type of acrobatics. And now I have to bring my friend and her kids back home. I was observing a once in a lifetime event that had to come to an end. And then that was it. I brought the telescope into the house and drove them home.

I returned as fast as I could. Oh, I was furious, to say the least. After all these years and writing this paragraph, I understand that I completely forgot to look for that fireball when I returned home. I remember getting back and getting out of the car. Slamming the car door and racing inside. I must have seemed like a pouting child, not getting his ice-cream because I slammed the screen door shut, went back inside, through myself onto my living room chair, but I forgot to look for UFO.

After I went inside, I jumped in my chair and exhaled. Then pondered, what else could it have been but a UFO? Was this the identical type of UFO the ex-wife, Roxanne, and I witnessed at Pipe Lake in 1975? Did they follow me to Phoenix? Or was all of this just coincidence?

Reflecting on it now, the characteristics of both fireballs were identical. Both UFOs seemed to be the same distance away from me. I do remember it being the same type. Meaning they looked exactly alike. Even though I didn't have a telescope to achieve a better look at the actual fire part of the UFO at Pipe Lake, they were both fireballs. Both seemed to be hovering around 150 feet up in the air and were about 100 yards away from me. Neither made any noise whatsoever. Both looked to be the exact same size, too. Of course, the fireball UFO at the cabin wasn't doing any acrobatics as far as I could tell. What are the odds of something so remarkable and out of this world to be happening like this? And for me to see two of them. Could this have been a coincidence?

I wanted to know more about fireball UFOs and if anyone else had witnessed these. I recently went to Wikipedia and looked up Ball Lighting and St. Elmo's fire, but nothing comes close to what we saw that day. I thought I could contact a scientist or someone to explain the fireball better. So I got someone who works in the field of plate tectonics and volcanoes. I thought they could help identify this object. I did contact some of them back in 1999, but they were no help, so I did a little checking into it myself. I know of no-fault lines near that location as some scientists say balls of fire accompany some fault lines as well as preceding earthquakes. I have never heard of an earthquake in the Glendale, Arizona so that one is out. Scientists also report ball lightning associating it to storms, but since this was a completely sunny day and maybe 108° degrees, that idea goes nowhere. Was it a type of plasma, and what exactly was on fire?

It's tough to wrap your mind around a UFO on fire or that some being, some extraterrestrial was inside that ball of flames. We humans still believe we're the only beings in the universe, so yea, this could be a UFO with an alien inside it, but really who knows?

And why did it perform those acrobatics? Again, who knows. I'm still searching for answers to these questions to this day. I'm inviting you all to help if you can. If you have witnessed anything similar and hope you have, come forward and contact me. My email address will accompany this book.

In the following chapter, my wife, Sharon, saw her first UFO, which pleased me greatly. She had always doubted that I see these things, but now she's a believer too. The gift worked its magic again. But this time they showed up in a swarm!

5

27 White UFO Orbs

"My own present opinion, based on two years of careful study, is that UFOs are probably extraterrestrial devices engaged in something that might very tentatively be termed surveillance."
Dr. James McDonald,
before Congress, 1968.

I stopped dating Kelsey after a year or so. I kept going to Club Central to meet up with my homies. When it comes to places in Phoenix where a person can hear some fantastic music and dance with lots of women, well, this was the place to go. Club Central is a great place to meet up with friends too because of the wide range of people. There was a mix of interracial people that would go there that were predominantly African American but also Latinos, Latinas, and some white guys, like me. Most of the women who came to the club, though, were African American, and specifically what I wanted.

These four guys I met up with every Friday after work were clowns and a lot of fun. A broad mix of friends, black, white, and Latino. It was a nice respite to complete the week of work and hear some R & B, which I prefer to listen to, plus do some dancing and have a few drinks to boot.

But I was getting bored, and I guess tired would be a better choice of word for what I was feeling. I was getting tired of dating women years younger than me. Tired of taking them out to eat and the conversation being somewhat immature. So, I took a break. My friends were begging me to come out for about six months. I kept telling them I would be OK sitting in my living room chair, watching a little television, and sip on a beer or two.

I've figured out that I needed to be by myself to get me healed emotionally. It can be challenging to work on oneself when there are others around. We need to work on our minds and all that comes with it. After about six months, I was feeling great. I guess I found the help I needed by being alone.

I finished another week of work, and I was driving back home. Then I get a call from one of my Latino friends, Dago. He's been calling for weeks, bugging me to get back out and get back to the way things were. He implored me to come out again. I emphatically told him NO! I wasn't interested. He said he and the guys missed me, and they'll buy me all the drinks for the night. Now, how could I say no to that? I told him, alright, Dago! I'll meet you and the guys at Club Central then.

We were sitting in our usual corner booth, which gave us the perfect spot to eye some women. We laughed and drank our beers when I noticed a couple of women walking up the stairs. One particular woman instantly captured my eye, and I rushed over to ask if she and her friend wouldn't mind sitting at the empty table next to us.

The girl I asked to sit next to me was named Sharon and quite the eye-catcher. Sharon is about 5 foot 3, 135 pounds, and shaped like a Greek goddess. Oh, my Lord, what a beautiful woman, and I was thinking, this girls got it going on. She asked her friend if that table would be OK. And she said to me, "Yea, we'll take it." I said great and escorted them over. I pulled out her chair, as any gentleman would, and she sat down. We instantly hit it off. It certainly didn't hurt that she was black and beautiful too.

Sharon and I talked and talked. I thoroughly enjoyed the conversation with her. However, after a couple of hours, I told her that my friends and I were going to another club. I was so excited to go to this new club that I completely forgot to ask Sharon for her number as I was about to leave. Sharon said, "Ah, do you want my cell phone number?" I said, oh, I'm so sorry, heck yea. So we exchanged numbers, and off I went. She and her friend decided to stay at the club.

I was thrilled with all aspects of Sharon. I didn't want to look too desperate, so I waited through the weekend to call her. I came home from work on Monday and noticed a message on my answering machine. It was Sharon, and she said, "A girl gives you her number, and you can't call her back? What's up with that?" How sweet. I knew then that she was pretty fascinated by me too. I instantly called her back, and again we engaged in a remarkable conversation. I had to learn more about her, so I asked her to dinner.

I told her that I enjoyed steak and lobster, and would that be OK? She agreed. I told her I would look for a place near her home. Sharon lived near the Phoenix and Tempe borders. On the other hand, I still lived in the mobile home, which was about a 30-minute drive from her. She lived relatively close to Arizona Mills Mall in Tempe, AZ. There's a place near the mall called Joe's Crab Shack. I called her back and asked if this place would be OK. She said "Yep. That would be fine." So I made reservations.

Sharon is an intelligent person and a lovely conversationalist. I enjoyed every minute with her during the meal. We dated for another year and a half, and I asked her to marry me. After the second divorce, I know I said that I'll never get married a third time, but that all changed once I met Sharon. I guess you can never say never.

She and I are so much alike, and it's almost scary. We have been married for over 16 years now. I don't know where I stop and where Sharon begins. I never thought I could marry my best friend, either. We're like spiritually conjoined twins.

I know now that I forced both those other marriages. I should have been true to my feelings about wanting an African American woman and shouldn't have married Roxy. And when it came to Christina, I was on the rebound, and she was the first thing I found. If you don't force things, the universe will take great care of you and bring you what you desire. I know that now too.

The next sighting happened in the winter, and it's the best time to be outside. The weather has finally cooled enough that we can start to golf and picnic and climb our mountains and so on. When it's 95 degrees here, it's like 75 degrees in Minnesota. The temps nearly every day from late October to late April are a beautiful 85 degrees. It's a great time to be alive.

It was a gorgeous Saturday, December 8, 2012, and the wife was inside watching television while I was outside on our patio laying in my lounge chair. I had my telescope up and running and using my Bushnell, 10 x 50 binoculars just looking around. My binoculars remain my most effective tool for viewing the stars and other things because I can just lay back and relax and watch some hummingbirds too. I put the binoculars down, and I looked south over to my left a little, right above my neighbor's house.

At that moment, I witnessed something and wondered, what are those? No Way! What are those balloons doing there? I jumped off the chair. My mind saw a bunch of white balloons, but on the other hand, were they a bunch of balloons? Sure, I thought these must be balloons. I kept staring at them as much as I could. If those are balloons, then I should be able to see one closeup.

When I first looked at them through the binoculars, I couldn't resolve an outline, unlike when I looked at them with my naked eyes. I could see round shaped white objects, but when I used the binoculars suddenly, the edges weren't sharp at all anymore, but how can that be? I thought, shouldn't there be an edge if these are balloons? It's exceedingly hard to explain because it's like looking at a cloud. You believe that there's an edge, but when you look at that with magnification, it trails off somehow. They were more illuminated towards the middle and less so at the outer edge.

I also observed them move for a few minutes to note how the wind was blowing them around. They seemed to be extremely high in the air, maybe a couple of thousand feet up. If you have ever been on top of a skyscraper, then you know how windy it can be the higher you go. Above our rooftops, a couple of hundred feet or so, the wind blows much harder than it does at ground level.

I said to myself that since the balloons are stacked up from maybe 2,000 to 3,000 feet up, the wind should be blowing at entirely different speeds. The higher you go, the stronger the wind blows. That's a given, but the entire stack of balloons moved at the same pace, slow, and that shouldn't be. And who releases a swarm of only white balloons, anyway? How could all those balloons just get away from someone holding them?

That's when it all struck me like a ton of bricks. WAIT A MINUTE HERE. These aren't balloons! These are those UFO orbs I've seen on UFO shows! You know when your mind is expecting one thing, and it finally shows you what you're actually seeing, well, it can come as quite a shock. This was exactly like when I was on the Mississippi, and I thought I was just looking at a flock of birds, and then I saw through them, and there were two gigantic round silver UFOs just hovering there. That was the same experience as this sighting because it blew my mind again.

After the confusion left mind, I yelled through the screen door to the wife, honey, could you come out here, please? There's a swarm of UFOs in the air out here. It took her a little bit because I talk about UFOs a lot. But this time, I possessed an extremely compelling reason to shout to her because these *were UFOs* or something. At least I knew they weren't balloons anymore.

She came out and said, "OK, Raymond, where are these so-called UFOs?" I pointed at them and told her, there, those are the glowing white orb UFOs people talk about on all those UFO shows. She excitedly said, "Cool, my first UFO sighting!" Then, we both just stood there, a little more than dumbfounded. We were looking at each other, then back at the balloons, then again at each other, and both of us had huge smiles on our faces.

I wanted to see if I could find a picture of white UFO orbs on the internet, so I went over to my laptop, which happened to be sitting on our patio table, and searched for some images. I hunted through a few pictures to obtain one very similar to what we were witnessing.

I brought the laptop over to her to show her the picture. I said, see, look, those are white orb UFOs as I was pointing to the screen. She said, "Oh my God, Raymond, they look just like those up there, as she was pointing at the orbs. Are we going to be OK? I mean, we're not going to be abducted or anything, right?" I said to her, I never heard of anyone talk about getting abducted by UFO orbs, so no, don't worry, honey. I've only heard people talk about orbs maybe flying around them, and under no circumstances did any of them make any threatening gestures. They just seem to be interested in people like gathering information or something, I said.

Sharon then said, "Well, what do they want, Raymond? What are they doing up there?" I replied, I don't know, sweetheart, let's just observe them for a while and see what happens. She said, "OK, but if they come flying around us on the patio, I'm going into the house, and you can stay out here if you want to." I said, no worries, Boob-A-Looba (one of my many pet names for her). I got you covered.

As we stayed outside and maintained a watchful eye on the UFO orbs, I would keep looking at them through both the binoculars then the telescope and still could not resolve the edges. I counted 27 in total, and we watched them for around 20 minutes. Unlike balloons at that height, the orbs never broke formation. During that time, they gradually went from the south side of our house to the west side. Each sphere was staying in the exact same spot throughout their journey. Not one orb moved away from any other orb the entire time either. Balloons just wouldn't do that. Balloons and wind *can't* do that. Each balloon would move up, down, and around all over the place because of the wind. That's why I instantly knew for sure these were not balloons but instead were UFO orbs.

What's strange about these orbs is they're witnessed more frequently by people. I'm not quite sure why it is this way, but many people have seen them. I continuously see videos on the internet from people in Mexico who are witnessing UFO orbs. I'm not sure if Mexico is a hot spot for UFO orbs or not, but there are many videos online from there. And it could be the fact that UFO orbs stay around longer, which means they'll be videoed more often too. It could also be that UFO orbs are devices such as our medical resonance imaging or MRI equipment that can check out biological beings and see what makes us tick. Of course, this is only speculation. I'm not sure of their true nature.

The UFO orbs never broke formation going entirely around to the west. Each sphere stayed at the same distance from any other sphere as they curved around the yard, and that just shouldn't happen. If these were balloons, they would be flying in and around each other. But the way the UFO orbs started was the way they ended up except for one very remarkable thing.

This is exactly what the wife and I witnessed.

I made this image in Photoshop. This is our backyard view on the patio and looking directly south, where the wife and I were sitting. Watching them and following the orbs as they leisurely moved from the south side to the west side of our home. I took a picture of our backyard and superimposed 27 orbs I created onto it. I can't say that I put each orb in its respective spot that we witnessed, but I did try to create what we saw. I had to make this image because both Sharon and I completely forgot to go into the house and grab our cell phones! I was thinking correctly and could have had a great video of them. Sorry about that.

Then something truly amazing happened; when they finally got to the west side of our house, they all just stopped, and there they stayed, never moving again. What I'm about to say will blow your mind because of what they did just after stopping. All 27 UFO orbs disappeared right in front of my eyes. When I was looking at them through my telescope, each sphere filled my eyepiece, which gave me a clear view of it. They seemed solid at one moment, and then I could see every UFO orb started to become ghostly very slowly like phantoms. For me, that was a mindblower for sure! It wasn't that they were shrinking in size. Oh, NO! It was how they looked. One minute each orb looked solid, then the next minute, they looked supernatural and faded away completely after a minute or so. This is the first and last time anything has ever disappeared while I was looking at it. Talk about otherworldly. This was it.

Sharon asked me, "Raymond, they look like they're fading away. Are they fading away?" I changed to my binoculars to better see them, but they all looked the same and told her so. I said, they seem to be fading away and not moving anymore, honey, but I can only see them disappearing when I look through the telescope. They're looking really weird now and might be gone all together soon. I don't know. "Where are they going, then Raymond?" she asked. I said, I just don't know, Sharon. She said, "Well, no matter where they're going, I'm just so happy that I could have my first UFO sighting anyhow." I was like, I know, right? This was pretty cool that you and I were able to have a sighting together. We looked at each other and smiled. They were slowly fading, and then they were gone, which took 2 - 3 minutes for them to disappear completely. Balloons don't fade away while you're looking at them, so I was convinced these were UFOs.

I wondered where they were going. Did they go into another dimension or something? I'm not sure about that, but wherever they went, they have never come back. Seeing those 27 white UFO orbs one minute and them disappearing the next is hard to wrap your mind around. When I say that it's hard for the mind to wrap your head around it, I mean it. How can something solid just disappear right in front of your eyes? I have never seen anything like it before or since that time.

When I see a UFO, I guess I'm in a kind of daze or frozen or something. I simply sit or just stand there as I watch the event unfold. I suppose it's because I don't want to miss a thing. I'm in awe every time something like this happens. Meaning every time a UFO shows itself to me.

There was one more thing about this sighting at the point when they all stopped. And I've never spoken of this until now, not even to Sharon. I remember the wind had died down, and I felt something, and it was eerie. I felt as if I was getting scanned somehow, like a light scanning across you when you're standing in the dark. It was a mysterious otherworldly strange feeling, that's for sure. I felt like they were trying to find out who we were and what this biological being is and how our bodies work or something. Maybe they were scanning our minds too. Of course, this is all conjecture, so I really don't know what was happening. But I did feel like something more was going on than us witnessing those UFOs. It was as if they were witnessing us too.

The very next day, I went to the National UFO Reporting Center or NUFORC.com to see a map of UFO sightings. And to see if anyone else near us happened to witness what we both saw. Based on data from the National UFO Reporting Center, their map allows you to explore the details behind over 90,000 UFO sightings dating as far back as 1905. I have gone there before and found some fascinating information, but I didn't see anyone else filing a report about this sighting. Unfortunately, it looks like it was only Sharon and me who were witnesses to this sighting.

I also went online to see if what we witnessed might have been something other than UFO orbs. I found out that there was a celebration going on simultaneously at San Tan Village. Here's what our news service AZCentral.com said about it: San Tan Village mall in Gilbert will host its first inaugural "balloon glow" event on Saturday. Entrance to the festival is free, and tethered balloon rides cost $15 to $25.

Balloon Glow: From 5:30 pm to 8:30 pm, 15 hot-air balloons will intermittently ignite their burners, producing a glowing effect. Other festival events include a kid's zone with a trampoline, train, climbing wall, hamster balls, and a mechanical bull.

We all want to understand what exactly these orbs are and if they are human-made or from another world. The news clip above mentions tethered hot air balloons, but since San Tan Village Shopping Center is almost 20 miles southeast of us, I very much doubt these could be those. They had gigantic hot air balloons, and I am virtually sure they were all various colors. I think that even if they lost control of all 15 of those balloons, by the time they would have made it to our house, they would have broken formation and definitely would have been considerably higher in the air than these orbs were. Not

A LIFE WITH UFOS

to mention that no balloons were ever released anyway, so they were not the hot air balloons from San Tan Village.

But where did they come from, and what was their mission, per se'? We must make sure that these orbs are not of this world. And if they're not from earth but some other planet, then from where? Or if they are from here, then what are they exactly? What are they made of, and who made them? And was I feeling that right about getting scanned? Have others felt like they've been examined by UFO orbs too? Or what exactly was I feeling anyway. Was the dead air sensation from the UFOs, or was it all in my mind? Remember that I told you that I had those similar mysterious feelings while witnessing the two UFOs on the Mississippi? Both sightings felt the same, unearthly, otherworldly.

But this sighting didn't come with that other feeling of being stared at by some being. I was lucky to see those orbs up in the air when I did. Fortunate that I was out on my patio at the same time. Luckily I had both my binoculars and the telescope working so I could see them close up. Lucky, or was it just a life with UFOs? I think the latter because it's happened so very often. I can't be that fortunate. I just can't be. They must want me to be there where they show themselves and to have other witnesses with me. But why?

UFO orbs are still a mystery and have been witnessed by tens of thousands of people for hundreds of years. If you don't mind, I would love to provide you a little history about UFO orbs I found fascinating. In Native American lure, specifically the Lakota tribes, they would speak of the Star People. They would have contact with mystical entities that came to them and were frequently perceived as orbs of light. They passed this information down through generations. Just how many is not known.

UFO orbs have been seen by white Europeans, too. Below is one such sighting hundreds of years ago. It has been written that in

July and August of 1566, something unusual had occurred in Basel, Switzerland. After this sighting, they created a broadsheet which represents a kind of news flash or pamplet of something grave. In the broadsheet are descriptions and depictions of what they witnessed.

The broadsheet states: *During the year 1566, on July 27, around 9 pm, the sun suddenly took a different shape and color. First, the sun lost all its radiance and luster. It was no bigger than the full moon. Finally, it seemed to weep tears of blood, and the air behind him went dark. And he was seen by all the people of the city. The moon, which has already been almost full and has shone through the night, assuming an almost blood-red color in the sky. The next day, Sunday, the sun rose and lit the houses, streets, and around as if everything was blood-red and fiery. At the dawn of August 7, we saw large black spheres coming and going with great speed as if they led a fight. Many of them were fiery red and soon crumbled and then extinguished.*

Here is a copy of the actual broadsheet. This is what they witnessed in 1566. Clearly, this was a sighting of a swarm of UFO orbs.

Creating a broadsheet meant that something exceptionally urgent needed to be written down and images depicted of what they witnessed. There is just no way for them to comprehend that these globes or what we currently dub UFO orbs could be ships from beyond our solar system. Just think about how people freak out about UFOs in today's world, much less over 400 years ago.

Unfortunately, our sighting was over after all 27 white UFO orbs disappeared. Sharon and I were dumbfounded and were in awe at what we just witnessed! We kept looking at the sky then looking at each other in utter amazement. Both of us had huge smiles on our faces. I said, that was awesome, dude! Sharon told me she had fun and wished she could see more UFOs, but unfortunately, this was her first and last sighting. I guess what she saw was good enough for the aliens or whoever was in those ships. And another thing; are UFO orbs ships or beacons or a scanning tool of some sort? Who knows. All I know is I'm happy being chosen somehow to have a life with UFOs. I wouldn't want it any other way.

The next sighting coming up happened just about a year after my orb sighting while I was outside again. This sighting was the gift working, and I absolutely could not believe what I observed in my binoculars. I love living in Phoenix because of what I will divulge to you next.

6

16 UFOs Above House

"This is the first sighting in Zimbabwe where airborne pilots have tried to intercept a UFO. As far as my Air Staff is concerned, we believe implicitly that the unexplained UFOs are from civilizations beyond our planet."
Air Commodore David Thorne,
Director of General Operations for the
Zimbabwe Air Force in 1985.

Since Phoenix has grown so considerably over the years, we have added lots of humidity into the air. More people mean more golf courses and sprinkler systems, more grass, more bushes and trees, and many more cars. This, by its nature, also represents more water in the air.

I read a study that our drivers put more miles on our roads here in Phoenix than Los Angeles drivers do, and we are one-third of their population. But it isn't the number of cars that cause the humidity to rise. Believe it or not, it's the number of golf courses because of the vast amount of water it takes to maintain that pretty green grass.

A few years back, a study was carried out by Arizona State University that showed how golf courses with grass had a higher average humidity level versus those courses with a desert landscape. The study included Phoenix, Palm Springs, and Las Vegas. It demonstrated a significant increase in humidity for those cities across the board with Palm Springs, showing the most substantial humidity increase.

A LIFE WITH UFOS

In 1974, I was in the U.S. Air Force and stationed at Davis-Monthan Air Force Base in Tucson, AZ. I wrote a letter to my mother about how pleasant the summers were there. I told her that the humidity level was only 5% when the temperature was well over 100° degrees, making it feel like an 80-degree summer day in Minnesota, where I grew up.

We've received an influx of people here in Phoenix since 1996, when I initially arrived. And with people comes the golfers, and we have an enormous amount of golf courses. Two hundred, to be exact! Because of this, the humidity has steadily gone from that low percentage to 30% and even higher every day now. Muggy and steamy does not come close to what we experience. Horrible is a more satisfactory term.

It's kind of bizarre here in Phoenix because the best parking spaces aren't the ones most adjacent to the store. It's the parking spaces under the most sizeable shade trees. To a large extent, when we come out of a store and get in our cars, we literally must wear gloves to protect our hands from the heat. Once I was even thinking of bringing my oven mitts. You can't touch the steering wheel in your vehicle even if you have a windshield sun protector up.

People here don't purchase cars with great heaters in them. They buy cars with excellent A/C units in them, and I'm not kidding. It's similar to when you have something in your oven, and you open the door, and whoosh, you feel that scorching air on your face. That's exactly how it feels here in the summer when you step outside.

But the winters here are so much better, and we can't wait for fall to come because we know that low temps are right around the corner. Many winter nights, I can stay outside for a long time because it's so cool. I love looking at the stars, and winters are usually the time to stay out and enjoy them. I can even write a book just like I'm doing now, and it's 6:00 am too.

Oh, how I love the fall and winters in Phoenix. The summer heat is mostly behind us and the night temperatures are way down below 80 degrees. I know that might sound high, but when you have nighttime summer temps over 105 degrees, 80 is nothing. There are nights in the winter where the temps are so low you can see your breath while outside.

The main problem we have during the winter is the number of drivers. We get an influx of people from the northern states flooding into Phoenix. We call them *snowbirds* because just like geese fly south for the winter, so do many northerners. The airports are more active, our roads are busier, and every major store is too.

And unlike Minnesota, that has fairs and such during the summer. We have fairs and festivals all winter long, from the State Fair in October to the Ostrich Festival in March. Before I got disabled, I used to go to many of them, but since then, I have curtailed most of that activity because I can't enjoy myself when I'm in pain. And walking around at a festival only adds to my discomfort.

Although I wake many times during the night from pain, I also can enjoy my time outside because of the lower temps. But there are some serious issues when I want to look at nighttime stars in the winter. There are many more cars because of the snowbirds, which causes a lot more car pollution as in smog. And our winter nights are usually choked with smog, which makes looking at the stars much more challenging. Plus, living on the east edge of Phoenix proper means much more light pollution from all the street lights, which drowns out starlight. I get hit with a double whammy when I'm trying to see the stars in my backyard during winter.

The temps were splendid on the night of this next sighting, though, and the skies were clear, which was very unusual. How wonderful it was to see the countless number of stars I could see, and the Milky Way seemed infinite. The central part of the Milky Way

Galaxy was right overhead and more than stunning. It was so clear out that I quickly found the Andromeda Galaxy with no trouble, too. And that was me using the binoculars! That was only because the snowbirds haven't come down yet, so I was enjoying the show, as it were.

Since my home is on the Phoenix-Tempe border, there's a lot of light pollution, and it's always best to use binoculars when I'm observing the stars. That's because I can see many more stars than I can with my naked eye when I have either my binoculars with me or the telescope up and running.

On the night of the sighting, I woke up early Thursday at 1:40 am. It was September 12th, 2013, and since it was in the fall, I was looking forward to an enjoyable time looking at the stars. Usually, after I wake, I do what I'm supposed to do and go right back to bed, but something was different on this night. That something was I had an overwhelming urge to go outside. I knew that this was the gift working, so I answered the call, as it were. I got up out of bed and made my way out to my patio.

When I go outside, I usually sit in my upright chair, but I decided to lay down on my patio lounge chair instead. I brought my binoculars with me and was looking forward to seeing a lot of stars. And sure enough, the stars were amazing!

When I'm looking through my binoculars, I mostly scan in a guided technique from horizon to horizon. I call it the "cutting the grass" pattern, which means I methodically look at the night sky going back and forth, just like cutting the grass in my yard. I start near the horizon, moving my sightline up from there. I move my binocular sight one eyepiece over and go down back down to the horizon. I usually go from my right side, cutting the grass and ending up to my left. I know I'm not perfect, but I try to cover as much of the night sky as possible to find any UFOs that might be lurking out there.

And this next sighting was a complete surprise, I thought at the time. But since it was the gift working again, I knew I was in for an excellent show.

As I was lying down on the patio chair and facing south, I was ready to start cutting the grass, as it were. I started scanning the sky from my right side to my left. I was looking as far right as I could, just above my neighbors' roof, when I noticed something coming from the west, and it was going to go right over me. Whatever it was, it was dark, and it was coming quickly. I started to get excited, and my heart was pounding. My mind started to race, and I was trying to figure out precisely what this was.

My first thought was, are those a flock of birds? But I knew birds usually don't fly at night, so I knew it could not have been birds. I was intently staring, trying to resolve what this thing was. Then I thought someone might have released a bunch of balloons, again because I noticed they were single round objects. But they were traveling much too rapidly. Balloons have no internal propulsion, so I knew they couldn't be balloons either. I was starting to get stumped because I couldn't make out exactly what I was seeing.

Then I made an extraordinary discovery. Whatever this was, it was triangular, which made me start to get really excited. I could make out a distinct triangular shape, but what exactly was this triangle?

Then it hit me. I was shocked! It's a UFO, I said to myself! I thought it might have been one of those black triangular UFOs flying overhead, you know, but then I saw a small round object, which I believed was a scout ship in front of the triangle and was dazed a little. I was wondering why one large triangular UFO would need a scout ship in front of it?

I then realized that this wasn't one triangular ship with a scout ship in front. This was 15 individual small, round, and dark gray

UFOs flying in a V formation with another ship, the scout ship, leading the way!

I witnessed something that caused me to finally understand what I was looking at and knew they were a cluster of UFOs and not one sizeable triangular craft. I saw a rectangular glow in front of each ship. But what was glowing, I thought? I wondered if this glowing was an instrument that allows these ships to navigate their surroundings or something?

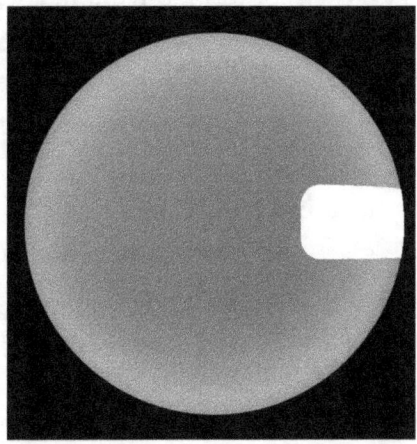

See the glowing instrument in front.

That glowing thing is what hit me like a ton of bricks! I said to myself, Holy Crap, those aren't glowing instruments, but windshields! You read that right, windshields. I understand how crazy that must sound, but it's God's honest truth. They all had windshields. I finally resolved that these were windshields because I could see the white curved wall inside the UFO. And I was stunned and absolutely stupefied.

Even though I'm outside looking for UFOs, my mind wasn't expecting actually to see any. How often would something like this go flying by right over my roof? I know I have a gift to intuit when and where to witness a UFO, but I was shocked once I saw that light coming from those windshields. It was a surreal sighting.

Once I realized these were 16 ships flying overhead, I immediately jumped up off the lounge chair to get a better look. I lost them for a second as I stood up and had to find them again with the binoculars. Luckily for me, I did so and quickly. It was unusually dark outside, and trying to see dull metallic gray ships even with binoculars was relatively difficult.

Still transfixed on their location, direction, and speed, I wanted to see them only with my naked eyes, so I dropped the binoculars down to my side. But I lost them again and had to relocate the swarm. I put the binoculars back up to my face and found them once again.

I believe these 16 round UFOs were single-pilot ships because they were so small, maybe 10 - 15 feet in diameter. They were just too little to be anything else, I thought. Just like the small bell-shaped UFO above the 7-Eleven, which I thought was a single piloted ship also.

I could see the entire squadron in my binoculars, although they did fill my view. I thought they must be very close to the ground if I could see them all and as well as I could.

I will try and estimate just how high up these UFOs were from me with what I witnessed in my binoculars. I can see an object or objects 100 yards or 300 feet wide at a distance of 1,000 yards or 3,000 feet in my binoculars. And presuming the ships were 15 feet in diameter and they looked like they were about one ship apart from each other, then the entire squadron was very close to me. Since I could see all the ships within the binoculars, this meant that the whole squadron was 300 feet or one football field wide and only 3,000 feet or 1,000 yards up! That's very close by for a horde of UFOs. Of course, all of this is guesswork, but I think I'm on the right track.

A LIFE WITH UFOS

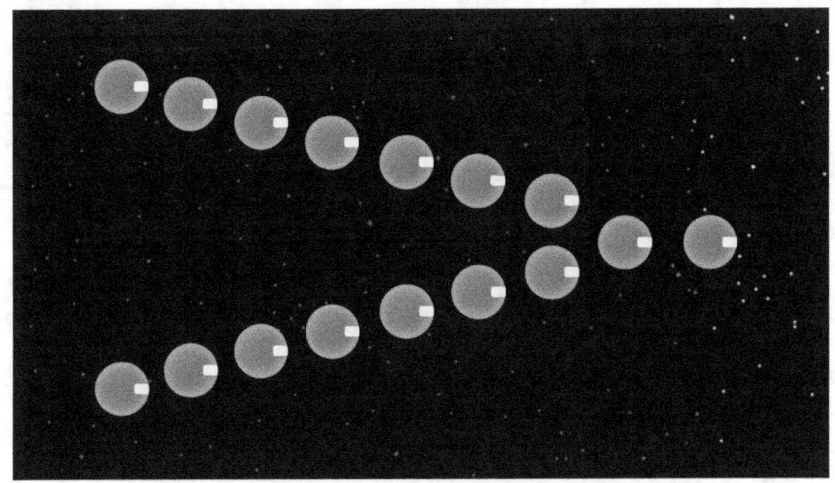

This is what I witnessed flying right over my house.

Although the image I made above shows the ships reasonably close to each other, they were, in fact, all about one ship distance from each other. That's how I deduced how large the swarm was.

At the exact moment of me standing there and shouting in my head, OMG, these are UFOs, and as if I summoned them to perform something, they then did something quite strange. Fifteen of them suddenly broke the V formation they were flying in and did some kind of acrobatics. That is except for the front ship, which I believed was a scout ship. The 15 UFOs started to go up, down, out, and around each other, looping this way and that. The acrobatics lasted about 5 seconds. Then they reformed right back into the original V formation directly behind the scout ship. It looked like three-dimensional bumper cars without any bumping.

Being in the U.S. Air Force, I have seen my share of jets flying in a V formation. But why did they perform the acrobatics right when I recognized them as UFOs? Was this a performance to screw with my mind because I realized what they were? Was this their way of hiding from me? If so, then why didn't the first craft do the acrobatics, too? Why did that ship keep flying straight?

I live no more than 6 miles south of Sky Harbor International Airport, which serves all of Phoenix. Maybe they did their acrobatics to screw with the radar signals from the airport. It's hard to believe they did this just for me.

My mind was racing to find answers to what I was witnessing. And why the windshields, I thought? I assume these were sophisticated craft with internal guidance systems, so why do the beings onboard need to look outside? Not only that, but why were they flying in V formation too? Canada geese fly in a V formation when they fly south for the winter to reduce the wind restriction. Why would UFOs need to reduce wind resistance, I also thought?

I was trying to figure all this out, and I can think of only one reason. These weren't spaceships at all, and they weren't extraterrestrial beings in those ships either. These were terrestrial training ships. Meaning, they were from our planet and not from some other solar system. It's possible they were on a military exercise of some sort but were most likely on a training exercise. Maybe they were learning how to maneuver these ships because the lead ship stayed in the same position while the others did the maneuver. For all one knows, there was a commanding officer in that ship, I don't know, but nothing else fits.

You see, when someone begins flight training to become a pilot, they usually start flying the plane by sight only. This is called VFR or Visual Flight Rules, and pilots cannot fly so high that they would be in the clouds. They need to see things like lights on the ground to navigate to their destination. They need those lights to determine where they are. They can't fly in fog either because the pilot can get confused and maybe crash. This is exactly what happened when John F. Kennedy Jr flew and crashed in 1999. He wasn't certified in instrument flying and couldn't tell that he was spiraling towards the ocean.

After mastering sight flying, the new pilot goes on to master flying with instruments only, which is referred to as IFR or Instrument Flight Rules. And that's why I think this was a training exercise because these ships weren't high enough off the ground to be in the clouds. It's called instrument flight because the pilot navigates only by reference to the aircraft cockpit instruments.

I started to take mental notes about the ships and anything that would help define them. All the ships were the same style—uniform color and diameter. There was no engine noise what-so-ever. I didn't see any more openings, and since they were so dull grey, I couldn't see if there were any cracks either. There were no markings on any ships as far as I could tell. It appears they were trying to fly incognito. Why else would they perform that acrobatic stunt? I asked myself tons of questions because a person of my age can forget things quickly, and mine is going fast.

There's also one troubling fact. We have Luke Air Force base here, which is directly west of my house. Luke AFB is 22 miles west of me, and these UFOs were on a direct path from there. Luke AFB is the most extensive F-16 jet training base in the world. F-16's fly Monday through Friday from 7 am to 11:30 pm, leaving 7 1/2 hours for other things. Maybe other stuff like UFO training? Maybe? Maybe not.

Being in the military, I have personal knowledge about how many radar dishes they have. And they have the most accurate and capable radars in the world. Assuredly, they would have detected these ships! Could they have been involved in some way? Could it be possible these were their ships on a training exercise? Who knows at this point, but it's a reasonable assumption.

The UFOs were high enough off the ground that both Sky Harbor International Airport and Luke Air Force Base radar operators could not have overlooked them. I believe both knew they were coming, and both knew they went through our airspace.

They first came into view nearly overhead but somewhat to my right, traveling from the west side of Phoenix, and were going straight east across our skies towards Mesa, Arizona. I followed them across the sky as best I could. The sighting lasted around 25 - 30 seconds, so I had an exceptional sighting. They performed the 3-dimensional bumper car acrobatics only once and for about 5 seconds. Then they reformed into the V formation.

I lost sight of them because they traveled far enough east that I could not see the lights from those windshields shining outward anymore. Sad to relate this, but the sighting was over. They blended into the night sky so well and were just too dark colored for me to identify them anymore.

When the sighting was over, I jumped for joy and was pumping my fist towards the ground, yelling, yes, yes, yes! I was so excited I scarcely realized I was shouting. There was no way for me to get back to sleep after that.

Consequently, I laid back down on my patio lounge chair and started cutting the grass again. I was thinking, who knows, maybe I'll catch sight of more UFOs. I'm not quite sure how long I laid there, perhaps another hour or two, but I knew I had to settle down. For the rest of the time, I didn't see anything else. I set the binoculars down and went back to bed.

Coming up next is a sighting so staggering in its breadth at what I witnessed that I was and am dumbfounded still. I might be the first and sole person in the world to see such a thing so unbelievable. Just the thought of it overjoys me to this day. It's hard to pick which sighting represents my fondest memory, but the following sighting is at the very top of my list.

7

UFO Flies Into a Wormhole

"I have frequently been asked why I think there is a cover-up (of) the facts about UFOs. I believe governments fear that if they did disclose those facts, people would panic. I don't believe that at all. There is a serious possibility that we are being visited by people from outer space. It behooves us to find out who they are, where they come from, and what they want."
Admiral Lord Hill-Norton, British Royal Navy,
Chairman of the NATO
Military Committee and former Chief of Defense.

This next sighting was on Tuesday, November 4th, 2014, and it was in the evening at approximately 6:00 pm. This time of the year is fantastic for viewing the skies because it's much cooler at night. And I was going outside to take full advantage of it. Thanksgiving was right around the corner, and Sharon and I were anticipating the holidays with the family. We were planning on having the Thanksgiving dinner at our house because Sharons' mom was visiting, and we were going to get the entire family to join us.

My mother-in-law, Syl Pope, was in town only a few weeks to celebrate the holidays with Sharon and I and the rest of the family. Back then, Syl lived in Alabama, in a small town called Equality, but now she lives in Scottsdale, AZ. She used to come once a year and stay with us. I loved it when she would come and visit us. Syl and I click on so many levels, as do Sharon and me. We inevitably enter into these deep conversations about reincarnation, spirituality, God, The Law of One, and the Ra material. Most of the time, we agree on almost everything we would discuss.

I had been observing the skies every night through my binoculars and seeing some exciting things. Like the last sighting of those 16 UFO craft flying in a V formation. That was one of the most spectacular sightings I have ever had. And I thought there was nothing that could ever compare to what I witnessed, but I was wrong, way wrong.

I kept going outside, sitting in my chair and looking to the heavens and hoping beyond hope that something would come along. I did see some UFOs above our atmosphere that I now call star-like objects doing strange maneuvers. I mean that there are star-like objects similar to satellites but aren't satellites that make U-turns, that stop or start to move, and things like this. I witnessed UFOs hiding out in plain sight above our atmosphere, unbeknownst to humans unless you happen to be looking for them. You will read an entire chapter devoted to these star-like objects. Satellites cannot stop or make U-turns. They are always on a direct path falling around the earth. If you think those points of lights you see at night are either stars or satellites, think again. They very well could be UFOs.

Most of the time, when I'm looking through my binoculars, I anticipate detecting a UFO, but usually, there's little to nothing but stars to see. When looking at the stars, most people only notice that they are just points of light, but there is so much more to them than that. I love looking at the stars because they come in many different colors and varieties. I can tell the difference if they're stars, satellites, the International Space Station, or UFOs. Well, most of the time.

If you don't mind, I would like to give you a little lesson about stars and binoculars. I do this because when you look at those points of light, you can, with what I am about to teach you to, tell the difference in those points of light to determine if they are indeed stars or maybe UFOs. And having a good pair of binoculars will give you a great view of a UFO, and I've had some stunning views of UFOs through my binoculars as in the sighting in this chapter. Stars range in color from blue to red, just like a rainbow, which also starts out blue on one side and goes to red on the other side and all colors in between. But rainbows are caused by sunlight and atmospheric conditions. Light enters a water droplet, slowing down and bending as it goes from air to denser water. The light reflects off the inside of the droplet, separating into its component wavelengths--or colors. When light exits the droplet, it makes a rainbow.

Rainbows come in all colors.

Stars come in different sizes too, but size has little to do with color. It's the temperature of that star that determines its color. Our sun is yellow because the surface temperature is around 6,000 F° or 3,300 C°. There are some stars like Rigel, a blue supergiant star that's only visible on winter evenings in the northern hemisphere and on summer evenings in the southern hemisphere. In our hemisphere, which is the northern hemisphere, Rigel is the first blazing star (lower right-hand corner) of the constellation Orion visible as the constellation rises. Rigel is so hot that it has a surface temperature of 28,000 F° or 15,500 C°, which is extremely hot, and that is why it's a stunning blue color. Rigel is over four times hotter than our sun.

Star Color and Tempurature Chart		
Color	Star Example	Surface Temp F° - C°
🔵	Rigel (Orion)	28,000 - 15,500
⚪	Sirius (Canis Major)	11,000 - 6,100
🟡	Sun & Capella (Auriga)	6,000 - 3,300
🟠	Aldebaran (Taurus)	5,000 - 2,760
🔴	Betelgeuse (Orion)	3,600 - 1,982

Star Color and Temperature Chart.

Things on fire change color because of the temperature of what's on fire. An example of color because of the temperature would be a cigarette match. If I were to light an ordinary match, I would see mostly yellow and a little red because it's only 1,300 F° or 700 C°. Another example would be a welders torch. They are a blue color because they're much hotter than a match. That's because an oxygen/acetylene torch is 6,300 F° or 3,500 C°.

I have included the image above showing star color versus temperatures to recognize stars a little better. That's why star colors range from blue to yellow and orange to red, and yes, there are bright white stars too. Now you know a little more about stars than you did a few seconds ago.

So when you go outside to look at the stars and hopefully be in a dark place, you'll see the different star colors. To me, seeing a star and its color always amazes me and always will. But also, you might identify if it's a star or maybe something else like a UFO.

Now let's go onto the subject of binoculars. I use the Bushnell 10 x 50 binoculars when I go outside to look at the stars. They are lower priced and within my range of affordability. I have another pair of binoculars, the Bushnell 20 x 50, that are twice as powerful to look closer at the moon, but I almost always use the 10 x 50's because they work well enough for me.

Binocular specifications are defined by two numbers, such as 10 x 50 or 20 x 50. The first number indicates the strength of magnification or how many times closer the subject is to you. The first number 10 or 20 means something is 10 or 20 times closer. The second number, like 50, is the size of the objective lens measured in millimeters going across the lens. The width of the objective lens will determine how much light the binocular can obtain for effective viewing. The higher the number, the larger the lens, allowing more light to pass through, thereby projecting a brighter image and viewing experience. Using binoculars gives me an edge when I witness a UFO. That's because I can see the craft closer to define its characteristics better. Or if you enjoy looking at the stars, I hope what I just told you helps you in some small way. And hopefully, you'll catch a UFO or two.

I not only love looking at individual stars but love looking at globular star clusters, nebula's, and old stars like Betelgeuse in the Orion Constellation. Well, at least in the winter, when the Orion Constellation shows up. The more you look at the stars, the more you will become familiar with where stars and clusters of stars are supposed to be. I will wager that a professional astronomer can tell if a light in the sky is supposed to be there or not. I can look at the Orion Nebula and determine if there is an extra star or two. Once I was looking at the nebula and witnessed several stars that just happened to start moving while I was looking.

This is a globular cluster and has hundreds of thousands of stars. Can you make out the different colors?

I was also outside when and noticed another star that I knew wasn't supposed to be there either. I was out on my patio, facing my large sliding glass door and looking around at the stars over my house. While using my binoculars, I noticed a very bright star overhead and a little to my right or southeast and directed my attention to it. This blazing star wasn't moving, nor was it supposed to be there. The star-like object was virtually pure white and unusually bright. There aren't many blazing white stars like this, and none were supposed to be where I was gazing. Again, just for an FYI. Sirius, another sun close to the Orion Constellation, is one of those blazing white stars and the brightest star in the sky. It's not that hard to find. Plus, it's always south in the heavens. That's why this so-called bright white star was so unusual, and I knew it wasn't supposed to be there, which instantly piqued my interest.

I knew, or should I say, I felt I needed to keep staring at that star in my binoculars because something was going to happen. And that something did happen. It started moving. The star-like object has instantly become a UFO because stars do not start moving. Only a UFO will.

I'm thinking to myself, OMG, another UFO! Very cool! I dropped the binoculars down to my side and outstretched my arm. I wanted to know how many degrees up from the ground the UFO was. I determined the UFO was about 45 degrees above the horizon. And it was southeast of my house or a little to my right.

It was moving my way towards my zenith or nearly above me, but not quite. I pulled the binoculars away from my eyes again and noticed that the UFOs path was curving towards me. The star-like UFO began slower than others that I have seen, but I could tell it was speeding up, but why was it speeding up, I wondered? I was also curious about why it would be curving. This was the first star-like UFO that I've witnessed that has ever curved, so now I was getting very interested as to why.

It took the UFO over 20 seconds to go from hovering at 45 degrees to 90 degrees nearly above me, and that's slow. Do you know why this seemed incredibly odd to me? Usually, when I see a star-like UFO start to move or is already traveling along above our atmosphere, they are nearly always going at a pretty good clip, but not this one, so I knew that this one was special. And I also knew it would be better if I had another witness.

So I opened the patio door to get the attention of my wife. I screamed into the house at Sharon and my mother-in-law, Syl. I yelled Sharon, Sharon, get out here quick! Come see. There's a UFO, and it's coming my way. The wife screamed back; "I can't come out right now, sweetheart. I'm making us dinner. I'll come out in a minute, Ray-Michele!" (that's one of the many pet names for me, and I call her Booba-Looba or Sweety-Peety) So I screamed at Syl then. I said, Mom, are you doing anything? Can you come out here, at least? I need a witness to this UFO I'm seeing! I'm not sure if she didn't hear me or was helping Sharon with the meal. Either way, she didn't reply back, and I was on my own. Unfortunately, I guess, Sharon couldn't drop what she was doing, so I kept standing there watching the UFO without the binoculars hoping she or Syl would come out.

As I stated earlier, I felt something was going to occur, but what? My expectations were going through the roof, as it were. Like when you're ready to open a Christmas present and the anticipation of what you might get. This was how I was feeling because I knew there was something special that was going to happen.

I put the binoculars back up to my eyes and watched as this star-like UFO was about to pass overhead and move to the left of me, putting it on a northeasterly projection.

While the binoculars were up to my eyes, I noticed some kind of light start to reflect in my binoculars on the left side eyepiece. It reminded me exactly like when I would view the stars and there's a full moon out. I would have the binoculars up to my eyes, looking at the stars but trying to find the moon. And when it's just barely out of view, I can see a kind of light reflection in my binoculars that's coming from the moon. Then the light gets brighter and brighter until I see the moon. That's what was happening as I was following the curving UFO.

Now I was getting pretty anxious because I knew that there was just no way that could be a reflection from the moon. After all, I knew that the moon wasn't out at that time of the month, so it had to come from something else. But what was that something else, I thought. What's causing this light reflection?

I pulled the binoculars away from my face and looked to see where the light was coming from, and there it was, a small circle of bubbling light—bubbling like a pot of boiling water! I was utterly stunned because I immediately knew what this bubbling light was, and I also screamed it out – OH MY FREAKING GOD, it's a wormhole, a freaking wormhole right there! I was SHOCKED and thrilled!

The wormhole was right in front of my eyes and nearly over my house too. Then I quickly looked over to the right at the UFO again and instantly knew why it was curving and speeding up because it's going to go right into the wormhole! And by HOLY GOD, I thought, I'm going to see a UFO fly into a wormhole!

How could life get any better than this, I thought! I said out loud with a long drawn out drawl; oh, so that's why I had that strong feeling like something BIG was going to happen.

The wormhole looked large in my binoculars and was somewhat round but looked more oblong from my angle. I extended my hand up, and it was around 3/4 to 1 pointer finger wide. Another example would be if I held a dime in my fingers and extended it out. It would almost be that size. Maybe that sounds small, but when you're looking at it through binoculars, that same small round object becomes very big. So I definitely needed my binoculars to unmistakably identify this object because I couldn't see it that well with just my eyes.

Once I could see this boiling light bubbling object, I could see that this had to be a wormhole because of the bubbling light part. There were light bubbles that were incredibly small down in the center, which made me realize that I was looking into a cone or funnel-shaped object. It was like an ice-cream cone without the ice-cream. What's weird is it had depth and no depth. I know how strange this sounds, but it's true. It looked flat because I could see stars right behind the opening, but I could also see smaller light bubbles coming up from deep inside too.

OK, picture this; you're holding an empty coffee cup extended out from your body. Turn it sideways or horizontal like you're pouring the coffee out, so the opening points to the right. Now tilt the opening a little towards you to see somewhat down inside the cup. Imagine if you took the coffee cup away, but the opening was still there. THAT'S what I saw but only made from bright blue bubbles of light. And THAT'S why I was so excited!

I started screaming at the top of my lungs for Sharon to come out. I said, Sharon, Sharon, there's a wormhole right over our house. Can you please come out? I shouted, Mom, can you at least come out? Mom cried back; "I'll be out in a second, Raymond." As soon as I heard her, I thought, in a second? This thing will be gone by then. What's a guy gotta do to get somebody out here anyway? I thought, oh well, I guess it's just me.

I was now confident I was looking down into a funnel. There was no mistaking this fact. The funnel was edge on like the coffee cup analogy above. There were smaller bubbles down in the center because the center of the wormhole was, in fact, farther away from my line of sight, which could mean the light bubbles would be smaller looking too. I couldn't see how deep the funnel was, but it looked considerably deep. The light bubbles were larger on my side of the opening. I assume all the bubbles were the same size and only seemed larger on my side due to my line of sight.

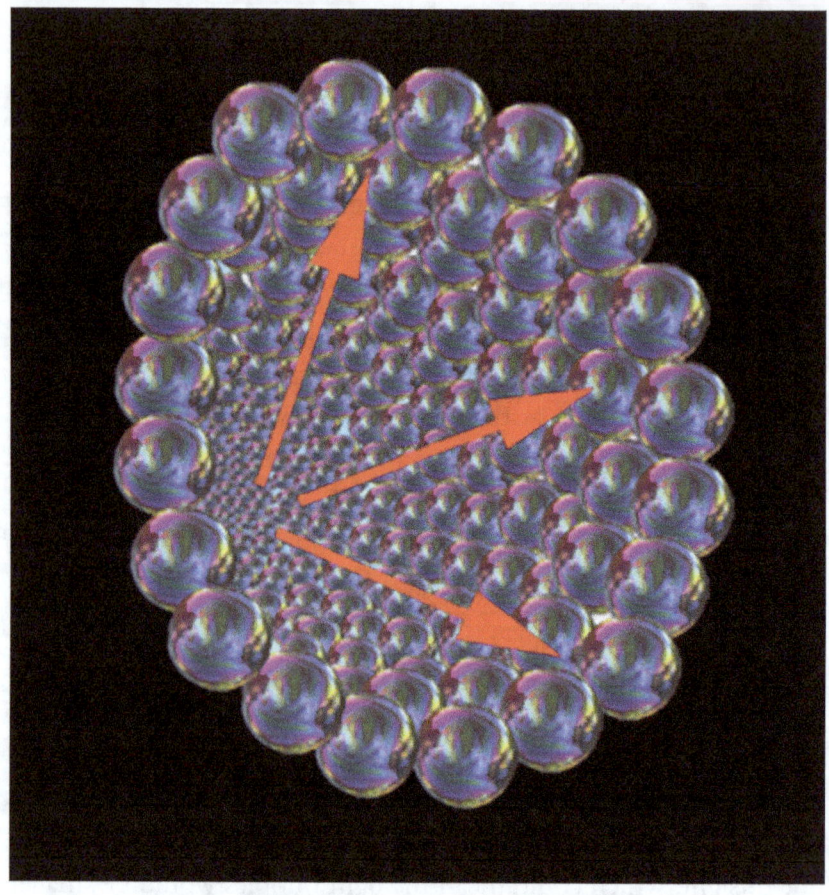

This is a depiction of the wormhole I witnessed. The arrows show the direction of the bubbles of light.

The picture above is not quite what I witnessed, but it's the best I could come up with in Photoshop. The bubbles were that size, with the larger ones nearer to me and smaller on the other side, but I couldn't get the right hue of blue. But it's very close to what I saw. I sincerely hope you can imagine or understand what I observed.

I took the binoculars away from my eyes and looked for the UFO. I noticed the UFO had just passed slightly overhead, going past my zenith, now heading northeast, or to my left. At that moment, there

A LIFE WITH UFOS

was no more doubt about what was going to happen. I knew it was heading for the wormhole, which was about another 10 – 15 degrees farther left.

The wormhole I witnessed was an extremely bright light blue color. The bubbles were made of light or from light, I guess. Not being a wormhole specialist, I'm only theorizing that they were made from light. But what could produce light on this scale, I wondered. I did see a very bright blue light emanating from deep inside, which made this object stand out. How could there be a wormhole right over my house? And how could I be the only witness in the world of something so extraordinary? Was this from our world, or was it an alien object?

I put the binoculars back up to my eyes because I wanted to enjoy this show up close and personal. I would go from wormhole to UFO and back again. The UFO was now a little farther to my left because it just passed overhead, and I could see the wormhole too. Then the UFO went directly into the center of the wormhole.

Then, something incredible happened. The instant the star-like UFO reached the center of the opening or the boundary from our spacetime into the wormholes spacetime, BLIP, the wormhole, just closed down or collapsed. I observed the wormhole close from the outer edge first and then shrink to its middle like folding a round piece of paper to its center. It took about two seconds to completely close. Then it was GONE! Both objects disappeared! It shrunk so fast that I couldn't believe my eyes.

The UFO was incredibly small compared to the wormhole's size and much smaller than the light bubbles, making the wormhole and bubbles seem huge by comparison. If I were to try and estimate the UFO and the wormhole's size, not to mention the light bubbles that made the wormhole would be extraordinarily difficult, obviously, but I'll take a shot at it; what if the UFO was a single occupant ship?

And maybe 15 feet in diameter? That would make each of the bubbles about 100 – 150 feet in diameter! And get this, the entire wormhole's width from side to side would then be somewhere between 1,000 – 1,500 feet in diameter! It's just a guess, of course, but it helped me fathom how enormous the bubbles and wormhole were.

After the wormhole closed down, I said out loud, WHEW! That was so freaking cool! I was standing there with the binoculars at my side. I didn't realize I was breathing hard as if I just completed a marathon or something. I couldn't move. I felt paralyzed at the thought of what I had just witnessed and the awesomeness of it all!

Then still standing there staring up for a couple of minutes, my mother-in-law, Syl, came outside and said, "What did you see, Ray?" I explained about the UFO and the wormhole, and she said, "Oh, well, OK, have fun then." I was thinking, have fun then, have fun then OMG mom, that was the experience of a lifetime! I don't think I'll ever get a chance to see another wormhole. And little old me might be the only person in the world to have seen it.

Thousands upon thousands of scientists study theoretical wormholes, and the universe picked me to see one. Amazing! I wished Syl or Sharon would have come out when I was shouting for them earlier. Or I wish I had a very sensitive camera that could record the smallest amount of light. If I could have made a video, I'm sure it would have gone viral! I am certain people would say the video is fake, but this is the absolute truth. I swear this is what I witnessed. I wasn't hallucinating, I wasn't dreaming, and I'm certainly not lying. You can give me all the lie detector tests in the world, and I will respond truthfully– I witnessed a UFO go into a wormhole!

Standing there, I'm thinking, so now what do I do? I was dumbfounded and in shock. But I did what I always did. I went inside and wrote it down, and this is my story—the story about the luckiest guy in the world to have this gift. The gift to intuit UFOs, and I guess

A LIFE WITH UFOS

that I can intuit wormholes too now. What a thrill it was to see a UFO going into a wormhole right over my head. Then it was all gone in a blip.

For some of you who are having difficulty understanding what all this wormhole stuff is, I'm going to break it down a little. Last night I was looking at an amazon television promotion and noticed an advertisement for a show. An image on the screen made me think about my wormhole incident and how this image could help people understand more about how a wormhole could represent a tear or opening in the fabric of spacetime. I took a picture of my T.V. screen and put it below.

Example of a tear or opening up spacetime.

As you can see from the picture that I took with my cell phone of the television screen that the woman is in her part of the universe peering into our side. That's what a wormhole is. It's a tear in the fabric of spacetime, creating a connection between two distinct locations of the universe, so when the UFO goes into the wormhole on our side of the universe, it could end up many light-years away or even on the other side of the galaxy. Just an FYI about the word spacetime; In physics, spacetime is any mathematical model, which fuses the three dimensions of space(width, depth, height) and the one dimension of time into a single four-dimensional manifold.

Albert Einstein's theory of general relativity allows for the existence of wormholes. Below is a depiction of Einstein's theoretical wormhole I made in Photoshop. It shows you what the passage through spacetime would look like and how it creates shortcuts for long journeys across the universe if they exist. I could only see into the right-side funnel.

A depiction of Einstein's theoretical wormhole.

I can say they exist now because I have witnessed and identified one! The UFO had to generate the wormhole somehow, but how? I've read that scientists believe that the only way to create a wormhole is with an almost unbelievable amount of gravity. So far, the only known way to create an object with that amount of gravity is with a black hole.

The definition of a black hole is a region of spacetime exhibiting gravitational acceleration so strong that nothing—no particles or even electromagnetic radiation such as light—can escape from it. The Theory of General Relativity predicts that a sufficiently compact mass can deform spacetime to form a black hole.

The only known black holes are in the middle of nearly all galaxies and not flying around and supposedly not above my house. At the center of our galaxy lies the supermassive black hole Sagittarius A*. This giant is about 4 million times the sun's mass and about 14.6 million miles (23.6 million kilometers) in diameter. An example of what this means is this; our sun is one million miles wide. Our galaxies black hole is only 14.6 million miles wide. That means putting 14 of our suns side by side and squishing 4 million of our suns in that tiny area—a tremendous amount of mass in one small space.

I just queried Google on how to create a wormhole, and it stated; In 2013, a group of physicists showed that by creating two entangled black holes, then pulling them apart, they formed a wormhole — essentially a "shortcut" through the universe — connecting the distant black holes.

Well, maybe for some wormholes, but I doubt I had two black holes 1/4 mile above my house. The gravity would have been so enormous that I would have been sucked off my patio and into them. Once scientists get a look at my wormhole, I'm sure they will have to go back to the drawing board, as it were, and re-figure wormholes created from black holes. I now know that they're made from light, not enormous mass. Maybe science has it wrong, and this chapter could show them how wormholes are actually made. For now, I'm going to have close this chapter of my life and wait until this book comes out. I'm confident the scientific community will contact me about what I've witnessed.

The following chapter is about a sighting that's so rare and spectacular that I was in awe of what I witnessed because of how close the UFO was to me. UFOs are never this close, and what I mean by close is it was just three houses down above my neighbors' backyard!

8

Black Triangular UFO in My Backyard

"In 1997, during my second term as governor of Arizona, I saw something that defied logic and challenged my reality. I witnessed a massive delta-shaped craft silently navigate over Squaw Peak, a mountain range in Phoenix, Arizona. It was truly breathtaking. I was absolutely stunned because I was turning to the west looking for the distant Phoenix Lights. To my astonishment, this apparition appeared; this dramatically large, very distinctive leading edge with some enormous lights was traveling through the Arizona sky."
Fife Symington,
Former Governor of Arizona.

The date was April 11, 2015, when I enjoyed another experience. It had been about six months since the wormhole sighting, and I was ready to see more. It was so fresh in my mind that it seems as if it happened yesterday. But now it's a new year and springtime in Phoenix. Spring might be what most people anticipate but not us Phoenicians because it's the start of much higher temperatures.

Some Phoenicians weren't anticipating what happened to them in the springtime, precisely on March 13, 1997. What happened was an enormous triangular UFO called the Phoenix Lights flew through Phoenix. Many witness accounts claim that the delta-winged UFO traveled from Las Vegas, Nevada, and slowly went down through Phoenix, passing over Tucson, Arizona. Finally, ending its journey with the last sightings in the Mexican state of Sonora. We live close to the Tempe-Phoenix border, and our home was near the path of the UFO. And although Sharon and I had been in Phoenix since the '90s, we didn't see that particular triangular UFO.

But thousands of people did witness the huge triangular craft and even a couple of people in our local government. One such person was councilwoman Francis Barwood. After reading some of the news reports by her, I was amazed at UFOs sheer size. She stated that she and her daughter were traveling down Interstate Highway 10, one of our state's major highways. The UFO went directly over her car as she was driving. She explained the ship was so enormous that she could still see the UFOs front and back if she were to take a newspaper and open it up over her head.

Many people had estimated that the UFO was over a mile wide. You indeed would have seen the Phoenix Lights, of course, if you were outside and looking up.

In the first place, it should NOT have been called the Phoenix Lights. There is a significant problem with this well-known sighting because the online video is not the actual craft, but flares dropped in a V-shape by the military. I have not seen any videos nor one camera picture of the real black triangular UFO that thousands of others witnessed.

It's profoundly interesting to me that the Air Force here just happened to drop flares in a V-shape near the time that the UFO flew over Phoenix. In later years, others saw more flares like the Phoenix Lights and thought the craft was again passing through Phoenix. And the military did what they seem always to do. They quashed those reports saying they dropped the beacons, and it wasn't a UFO.

Different triangular UFOs and human-made delta-winged jets.

There have been other UFOs witnessed that have been triangular shaped as in the image above. A sailor took the top left picture while he was manning a periscope while stationed on a sub. He saw the UFO and snapped a few pictures. I believe with his cell phone. The top center is a recreation of the Phoenix Lights sighting that thousands of people witnessed. And the image to its right was a small triangular UFO someone saw and recreated that one too. Of course, all three bottom images are human-made delta-winged jets.

Did the Air Force know that an enormous UFO was coming through Phoenix? I'm sure of it. I genuinely believe they had prior knowledge that the ship would go through Phoenix and needed to conceal it by dropping those flares as a decoy. And they were trying to suppress any rumors and gossip about UFOs. Maybe they were trying to save people from getting terrified at seeing a UFO.

Who knows, but the timing is just too coincidental. Besides getting a heads up, could the Air Force have seen this gigantic triangular UFO on their radar? You can stake your life on it!

A few years ago, a courageous man came forward to talk about Air Force radar and what the military knows about UFOs. He was in the Air Force and trained as an Air Traffic Controller. I believe the story goes like this; this man joined the Air Force and became an Air Traffic Controller on a base in Oregon. He came into work one night at the air traffic control tower and noticed many people huddled around one of the screens. This man was a bit baffled about the goings-on, so he went over to the screen to see for himself. He looked at the screen and asked someone what was happening. Another Air Traffic Controller told him to take a look for himself. It's a UFO!

There were other Air Traffic Controllers and higher-ranking officers there too. Even the ground people were there; these are workers outside on the tarmac, loading baggage into planes and removing the chalks from airplanes' tires and such.

This gentleman was a rookie, and he started to freak out. He asked his commanding officer, who happened to be there, "Who do we contact about this, sir?" His commanding officer said, "Well, no one, son. Listen, you don't call anyone, and you don't log this either. And you don't speak to anyone like the press about this. Do you understand me? This is above Top Secret." He came up to him, spoke louder, emphasizing each word, "NO ONE IS TO KNOW ABOUT THIS!" He continued, "Regardless, NORAD will handle this son, so they'll take care of it." He asked his Commanding officer what he meant by this. The officer said, "Sometimes before a UFO comes into our airspace, NORAD will call us to give a heads-up so that nobody will freak out."

If you don't identify what this acronym NORAD stands for, it's the North America Aerospace Defense Command in Colorado.

They are here to maintain the continuous capability to detect, validate, and warn off any atmospheric threats for the entire United States of America. It sounds like they also watch for and verify UFOs too.

This poor guy was so frightened at that moment. He stood there, watching the screen with everyone else. Seeing this unidentified blip on the screen, he wondered how it could be like this? Don't people need to know? Wouldn't this be like the 1947 Roswell incident, where the Air Force found a downed UFO? He had so many questions and nobody to ask. Was this standard policy in the Air Force? What was happening was a craft of unknown origin that came into his airspace, flew through it, and disappeared. His superior ordered him to do nothing because NORAD had this. And this wasn't the only time that a thing like this occurred.

It has come to light that something like this has happened before. Air Traffic Controllers receive calls from people about witnessing a UFO all the time. If another UFO was seen by the police or the public and contacted him, he was ordered by his commander to use a canned response; nope, we haven't seen anything on our screens. Or nowadays they say, contact the (DoD) or the Department of Defense.

Throughout the years, that was the only thing he could think of, those dang UFOs! People just have to know, he thought. He concluded that since he was out of the Air Force for a couple of decades that he better come clean and tell the truth and maybe save his soul from all the lies.

He was always terrified of being classified as a whistle-blower and the trouble that comes with that title. His conscience was getting the best of him, though. Consequently, that's what he became, a whistle-blower. He went in front of a news reporter and camera, giving about a thirty-minute confession on the entire ordeal. To him, not telling the truth to the public was an enormous lie. He thought he needed to right this wrong.

Why aren't there more whistle-blowers like this brave man? There are various reasons why most people in the military or commercial pilots don't blow the lid off the UFO question. One reason is the threat to family and friends. And many people have been threatened if they have seen a UFO and want to tell others about it. And this poor guy is most likely the issue too because you rarely hear a whistle-blower come out when they're currently in the service. Military and private pilots believe they could lose their positions, which they have spent many years of training to obtain a pilot's license. Most pilots became this because they love nothing else.

The days after the massive triangular UFO flew through Phoenix brought fear among the citizens. They were looking to the local government for answers. It would have been prime time for our local government to step forward and demand our federal government tell them and us what was going on.

I believe our local government should have taken the reins and initiated a serious investigation of UFOs because so many people who had witnessed this UFO were terrified at the thought of it flying over Phoenix. The phone lines were jammed. People were calling whoever and trying desperately to find someone somewhere that would relieve their anguish. The government positively could have done more than they did because what they did was shameful.

We Americans are a strong-minded people. Whenever something serious comes up, I think that's when we shine above all others on this planet. We don't cower down. We stand straight, pull up our sleeves, and do what it takes to alleviate the trouble.

Instead of taking this seriously, our governor thought it prudent to make light of the situation to calm people down. The day after the UFO came through Phoenix, our elected official, Governor Fyfe

Symington, did something terrible at a press conference and poorly handled the situation. He had one of his staff members dress up like a gray alien and come out on stage!

Sightings of UFOs are a significant situation, and like so many other government officials before him, he made a mockery of this momentous moment. Most of the reporters started laughing. He was asked point-blank by a journalist if he witnessed the craft but denied any sighting. It's troubling to me that he made light of such a fantastic event like this.

Governor Symington made the quotation at the beginning of this chapter some years ago after he was no longer governor. I'm convinced he did it to calm people down. And I'm sure he was equally nervous he would lose the next race as governor if he came clean about his sighting.

The Phoenix councilwoman I talked about above, Frances Barwood, lost her job the next time she tried to run for re-election. The public ostracized her for telling the truth, as is the way many people handle something so unknown. They think the person who witnessed something so extraordinary must be crazy and not trusted anymore.

I would like to semi-quote the governor again, so you can understand what I'm trying to say. "I saw something that defied logic and challenged my reality. I witnessed a massive delta-shaped craft silently navigate over Squaw Peak, a mountain range in Phoenix, Arizona. It was truly breathtaking." As you reread this, you understand Governor Symington witnessed the same UFO many Phoenicians and others witnessed. His sworn duty was to serve and protect. He neither served us nor protected us well. Because our governor made light of this critical sighting seen by thousands of his constituents, he missed a crucially significant opportunity.

It was his duty not only to listen to but act on that incredible sighting, and he didn't respond well. That's what I believe. He has since apologized for his actions, but only after being voted out of office. He understands he did not handle the situation appropriately. I guess I can forgive the governor. But I'm equally sure that if something like this happened in Phoenix again, history would repeat itself. It's all about not being seen as a nut.

And this is precisely why most people will not say anything about a sighting of a UFO they had. People are made fun of for what they witnessed. Witnesses are harassed and misjudged and looked at as crazy, even by family members. I can attest to that. Most of my family think I'm a lunatic and don't believe I've had a life with UFOs.

For example, after the wormhole sighting, I talked to several physicists about what I witnessed, and all of them told me I must have hallucinated it. I was quite awake and lucid, I can assure you of that. Was I hallucinating? Really? How many people do you know that one minute their fine and the next they're hallucinating? Especially without taking any kind of drugs like LSD. I don't know anyone that has ever done that! After explaining to those physicists about the wormhole, I thought this would have been an excellent opportunity to want to know more and perhaps study the phenomenon. It might have opened their minds and more than helped their careers to new heights.

OK, I'll stop complaining. As the statement goes, bitter, party of one, your table is ready. I know that the governor and those scientists are just trying to rationalize what they think is normal, but they seem to hit a wall of ignorance beyond that. And I'm still not sure why. I can say I was ignorant, too, when it came to my gift and the life I've been given.

But I can say now that I was up that night due to the gift. Most of the time, after I wake up during the night, I do what I need to do and go right back to sleep. This time I felt a strong urge also to go outside to look at the stars. It was early morning, 5:50 am. Sunrise was only 10 – 15 minutes away, but it was still light out.

I was standing in my yard facing south, panning my binoculars left to right near the horizon. You know, cutting the grass? And, I had that feeling again. Someone somewhere was staring at me. But this time, it felt unusually strong as if there ten people surrounding me, hiding from sight in every nook and cranny.

With the binoculars still up to my eyes, I was trying to figure out just where this powerful feeling was coming from, then suddenly, blackness filled my view. I was like, what the? I dropped the binoculars down because, at first, I thought I was seeing the side of my neighbors' roof. I was more than stunned at what I was looking at and screamed to myself, OH MY GOD, A BLACK TRIANGULAR UFO! And it was coming my way! I couldn't believe it, I thought, it's going to fly right over me. It was so close to me that I couldn't use the binoculars, so I dropped them down by my side and only looked at it with my eyes.

At first, the ship was heading north towards me. The UFO was going very slow, maybe 2 or 3 miles per hour. The craft was jet or flat black like our stealth bombers are colored. I've also read some UFO books about UFO witnesses seeing flat black helicopters accompanying their sightings, and I thought it looked a little like one of those because of it being matte black. I was so shocked at seeing it that I was more than confused at first and couldn't appreciate what it really was. A black triangular UFO in MY neighborhood!

I was astonished because the UFO was only three doors down, nearly above my neighbor's roof and clearly over their backyard. Maybe 50 to 100 feet off the ground, and that's close. But why was it so close, I thought? What are they doing here? Or maybe what are they going to do? I'm not really worried about being abducted, but I wondered why they're so close to me? Were they here for me to witness them, or was this an unintended sighting? Or were they dropping somebody off?

I was amazed not only by its closeness, but the sheer size of the UFO was remarkable! I thought the craft to be somewhere between 75 – 100 feet in length. I used to fuel up helicopters in the Air Force and know they are around 57 feet or 17 meters long, and this is how I estimated the length. Like two helicopters tied together.

It didn't seem to be a single occupant UFO, but more like it had several beings onboard. Maybe that's why I felt the gift working so intensely. I knew several people or creatures were staring down at me. I felt that there were many eyes on me at once. As if there were maybe 5 or 6 of them all watching me. This time was the only time the gift felt eerily fervent. Just how many beings were on board is still a mystery.

I could see the tip of the black triangular UFO. It looked sharp, similar to the tip of an arrow, pointing right at me. I stood there staring at this UFO for something like 10 – 15 seconds, thrilled that it was going to go right over me. I also thought, why is it coming towards me? Never before or since has a UFO traveled towards me. The thought of being abducted did cross my mind. But thankfully, UFOs have never made any aggressive moves towards me, so I wasn't apprehensive, but who knows?

As it was coming towards me, I noticed a light on the underbelly. It was high enough off the ground that I could see that it had a sizeable glowing round red light in the front of the ship just behind the tip. The red was a deep red rose color. All our planes come with bright red navigation lights, but this light was nowhere near as bright but dull. There was a tree blocking my view of the ground, so I couldn't see if it was shining down on the grass or not. Other UFO witnesses have observed ships doing this. They may be analyzing earth's ground cover, but who knows?

Being transfixed on this UFO, I suddenly thought; I need to run in and get my phone to snap a bunch of pictures. Right then, as if the beings on board heard my thoughts and didn't think it prudent for me to take any photos, it instantly turned right. That's when the UFO started heading away from me.

Once it turned, I could see how close to the rooftops it was. Knowing all the houses in our neighborhood are similar in size, I could see the ship's side and estimate its thickness, which I thought to be around 10 - 12 feet. The UFO looked very thin compared to its overall dimensions.

The UFO was an isosceles triangle variety. There are different types of triangles, of course, and what I mean by this is the UFO was not an equilateral or scalene type but an isosceles triangular shape.

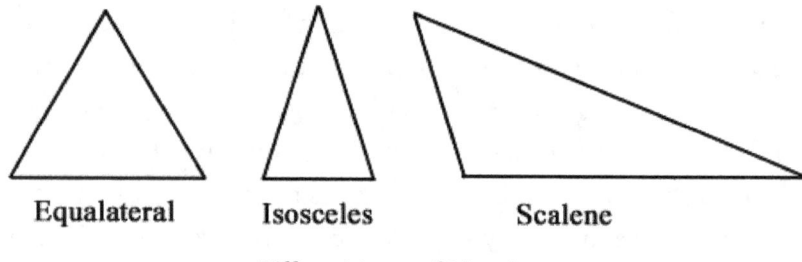

Different types of triangles.

When it turned to the right or west, I could see there were no windows or cracks. There wasn't any sound or humming noise associated with it. I felt no static charge, as some people have said about their sightings. There weren't any markings anywhere I could see on the UFO, as all our planes have. The craft turned so casually that it seemed like it did not care if I was there or not, so why leave? Why wouldn't they allow me to get my phone to take pictures?

This is exactly what I witnessed as it was leaving.

Then the UFO took another right turn heading south, which unfortunately was going away from me. Once it turned for the last time, I could see the back of the UFO and estimate its width, which I thought to be about 50 – 75 feet wide. That's when I noticed the two lights on the back panel of the craft. They were both yellow and each near a corner. Just as if they were two engines or something. The yellow was close in color to a dandelion yellow, and none of these lights were exceptionally bright either. Again, just a dull type of light. And, if the ship were 10-12 feet thick, that would make both the yellow lights on the rear of the UFO somewhere around 8-10 feet in diameter. Those are huge lights!

What could be their purpose, I thought? I am not sure why the UFO had those three lights on it or why they were different colors. UFOs are here for a reason, and I think most UFOs are here on scientific missions about our planet and us. Everything on a UFO has a purpose, as do all things on our aircraft.

What was so strange about the UFO turning was I never really saw the turn part. Before the first turn, when I thought of getting my phone, I blinked, and right then, the UFO was now facing west. At the time, I said to myself, that was weird. How did I miss the craft turn? I watched it for 2 - 3 seconds more while it was in that direction and blinked again, and the ship had somehow turned again and was facing south away from me. Now I knew there was something fishy about this craft. Yea, I could have missed one turn, but certainly not both.

There had been rumors floating around the internet that some of these flat black triangular craft are actually holograms masking the craft's true nature. Those people believe that our government has created secret helicopters. Could they be showing me a matte black triangular UFO and hiding a classified soundless helicopter somehow? Could this have been one of those? And why hide behind some type of cloaking device? Isn't a UFO just as fantastic? Was I some sort of test figure being in an experiment or something? I don't know, but what I do know is this was one crazy sighting!

If I had not come out at the exact time I did to look at the stars, it surely would have gone right over my patio. But it turned away from me and slowly flew out of sight, I think, and it was gone. And here's the kicker about that; once the ship was completely hidden behind the tree in my next-door neighbors' yard, I blinked again, and I never saw the craft anymore, just like it popped out of existence or something. Again, like it was a hologram or game object, my kid would play on our television, and someone just turned the T.V. off.

I thought, dang it; it's taking off, and I was so bummed and joyful at the same time. I knew I did not have enough time to get my phone and was mad at myself. But I was also wondering, where did it go? If it were going away from me as slow as it was coming towards me, then I should have seen it shrink in size as it traveled down the yards, but that's not what happened. Again, poof, it was gone.

Because of that dang tree blocking my view down the block, I would have seen where it went or even if it just disappeared. I quickly got up on my patio lounge chair, standing as high as possible, and extending my head and neck as high as feasible, but the craft had left by then. I have a front gate on the east side of my house and ran over there to look, but I didn't see the UFO anymore. I don't know where it went and realized that my heart was pounding out of my chest. And I was jumping for joy and screaming, yes, yes, yes! Then I regained my whits because I realized I was shouting at the top of my lungs, and it was still before 6 am. I put my hand over my mouth like a kid crying out in church and whispered, yes, yes, yes. That was so cool. For days I had a smile on my face.

I was thinking about this UFO and wondering what were they doing in my neighborhood and why? It was 5:50 am as well. Many people in Arizona get up close to that time, so it was more than a little risky for them to be here then. Were they dropping off an abductee? Were they here to pick me up? Alien abduction is a real thing. It has happened to millions of people worldwide. Something like 1 in 50 people has either been abducted or know someone who has. Why else would a UFO be that close to a house? Studying our roof composition, I wouldn't think so. Plus, there is nothing special about the homes or land around me. It's just an ordinary middle-class neighborhood, and there's nothing much else to see.

This sighting was by far one of my favorites because it was so up close and personal. When I first witnessed it, I was praying it would come right over me, but of course, they had other plans, and now the UFO was gone. What a sighting, I thought, though! As I explained in the introduction, this was a major sighting, as in; an actual craft that I can define their characteristics like, how big, what color, etc. So far, this was the last time I had a major sighting, but I'm hoping for more. I'm due since it's already been six years since this sighting.

The next or last chapter will be on minor sightings. A minor sighting is about star-like objects. Because they are near or above our atmosphere, the only thing I can define is they are points of light. Yes, they're UFOs, but what type? That's why I put all the star-like UFOs into one chapter.

Coming up, I will discuss some very odd stuff about the early mornings here in Phoenix. We seem to have a time when most people are asleep, and there's a lot of UFO traffic buzzing all around us. Since most of us are not awake, we never really notice what's happening. I call this time the bewitching hours and if you are ready, let's go to the next chapter.

9

These are not Satellites or The Bewitching Hours

"Something is going on in the skies... that we do not understand. If all the airline pilots and Air Force pilots who have seen UFOs and sometimes chased them...have been the victims of hallucinations, then an awful lot of pilots should be taken off and forbidden to fly."
Captain Kervendal,
French Gendarmerie.

I want to tell you something about this chapter. You will be reading about star-like objects only, which I call minor sightings of UFOs I spoke of in the introduction. I call them minor sightings because they are not a physical craft that I could describe other than being points of light. The dates of these minor sightings intertwined (2011 - 2019) within the major sightings, meaning the dates you will read about happened before, during, and after some of my major sightings. Since these star-like UFOs are the same UFO type, I wanted to keep them in a single chapter. These are in chronological order too. I hope this won't be too confusing.

You don't need a fancy computerized telescope to catch these UFOs where you live. You only need some manner of eye enhancement apparatus like binoculars. And they don't need to be expensive either. My binoculars were reasonably inexpensive, costing less than 30 dollars, and with them, I've seen all the UFOs in this chapter.

I am calling this chapter "These are not Satellites" and "The Bewitching Hours." The reason is that although the stars up in the nighttime heavens seem to be your typical suns many light-years away, some are not stars or satellites or even the ISS (International Space Station). That's because UFOs hide in the open. They know the average person cannot determine which is a star or which a stationary satellite, so they park up there in plain view. It's only when one looks at them, and they start to move, or they make an unusual movement like a U-turn that one realizes they're a UFO, and I have seen these many times. In Phoenix, Arizona, at least, there is a tremendous amount of activity in space all the time. I can't tell you if this same phenomenon is happening elsewhere or not since I have only seen this happen in my neck of the woods. But you can bet your life that it's occurring right above you too.

Now you know why I could call this chapter "These are not Satellites," but wait, what about the other title you might ask? The definition of bewitching is to cast a spell on or take control over someone. When I refer to this chapter as the "Bewitching Hours," I mean that part of the alien plan, I believe, has been the control and abduction of humans over time. These so-called stars or UFOs are up there in the night sky for a reason, and it's not because our planet is so beautiful. It's most likely to take control of us humans.

I have witnessed many of these UFOs take off between 3:00 a.m. – 5:00 a.m. But where do they go after they get done with what they're doing here in Phoenix? And what exactly are they doing here anyway? I don't know, but some have come down to the planet from above the atmosphere, and I have seen this too. Maybe that's when they come to do scientific experiments on our land. Perhaps for abduction reasons, again, I don't know. Both titles are apt to work together because you cannot have one without the other; it seems. I will explain more about this below.

When I think about how many people worldwide have seen a UFO or have been abducted by UFOs or aliens, it staggers my mind. The prevalence of these beliefs is unknown, but estimates vary from at least several thousand worldwide to 3.7 million in America alone. I took these figures from three national surveys conducted by the Roper Organization. It seems to me, at least, that there must be tens of thousands of ships out there. If not, then there are some very busy aliens.

And when I say, out there, I mean just look to the night skies. That's where they hide in plain sight. And that's one of the problems I've noticed. When I see people walking around, many are looking down at the ground or looking straight ahead. Let me ask you a question. How many times do you look upwards? I know we need to look down so we don't trip over anything. I'm talking about when you're sitting down relaxing. That's a great time to look up and around because you can catch a UFO or two. For me, too, because if it weren't for the gift working, I would miss a lot of sightings.

One reason any UFO would be here is to abduct humans and or do scientific experimentation on them. They also come down to the surface and do testing on our planet, I believe. But they have to wait for the right moment. And that's when they can come down, under cover of darkness. And after they have finished with those abductions or whatever they're doing, they take off. I always see a lot of UFOs leaving our skies around 3:00 a.m. – 5:00 a.m. It literally starts at three in the morning, lasts until five, and then stops like turning off a faucet. I rarely see any more traffic across our skies after that.

Of course, I have witnessed ships during the daytime, which could mean they are just finishing up those experiments. Like the last chapter about the black triangular craft that was in my neighborhood at 6 a.m. Why were they in our backyards at that time? Was I going to be the abductee, or were they dropping someone off? I guess I'll never know for sure, but the timing was just too consequential.

So once they leave, you might ask, where are they going then? I believe they are going to another nighttime place when it's daytime here. As an example, I am writing this page at 10:00 a.m. Phoenix time and in Perth, Australia, it is 8:00 p.m., so they could be leaving from here and going to another area of the earth that is nighttime. I'm not saying that they are going to Perth necessarily. I'm just giving that as an example because of the time differences.

The problem I have is proof or the lack thereof. Most of these UFOs are not in our atmosphere, they are up in space, and in space, a UFO looks exactly like a star or a satellite. And satellites look like points of light. They emit a white light unless seen near the horizon, where they can appear yellow. But all in all, they look like any other sun when they're traveling around the planet.

What distinguishes UFOs from stars or satellites are their movements—like an earlier chapter of the UFO curving into a wormhole, then disappearing right in the middle is a prime example. Satellites do not curve. They go on a straight line across the skies. But when you see a point of light you think is a star and it starts moving is another prime example. Or on the flip side, when you see a star-like object, and it stops moving, then it's a UFO. These are not satellites but become UFOs because satellites can't stop moving. Only a UFO can.

Stationary lights in the skies, as well as moving lights, have been witnessed since time immemorial. In ancient Hindu scripture, written in early Sanskrit, there is an ancient religious text called the Vedas. Part of the Veda scriptures is the Mahabharata, which is one of 2 epics or narrations of a legendary figure or figures. In this very epic, there were flying celestial ships that were also perceived as stars.

Back then, the people used to call them lamps in the sky. They did not know what a star was; therefore, they used their own vernacular to describe what they witnessed. They referred to UFOs as flying chariots, celestial vehicles, religious events, and other things.

In the Mahabharata, they stated there were thousands of them beyond the moon. The ancient east Indians were even invited to fly on those ships, and they witnessed many battles among them. These ancient texts have not been accurately dated, but scholars think they could be written between 1000 - 1500 BCE! So seeing star-like objects has happened for thousands of years.

There is an excellent book about that very subject, The Chariots of the Gods, written by Erich von Däniken, who is arguably the most widely read and most-copied nonfiction UFO author in the world. I would recommend you pick up his book, which is published by Harper & Row. Either way, ancient Hindus claim to be star people, as have many other cultures worldwide.

On to my sightings of star-like objects then. My wife let me buy a new telescope some years ago. I purchased it and wanted to do some astrophotography with it. This means I can take images of whatever might be in the night sky like nebulas or globular clusters. These are densely packed balls of stars. Globs, as I call them, can easily have more than 100,000 stars packed in them, and they are my favorite thing to look at in the night skies.

The closest star to us is Proxima Centauri. It's about 4.22 light-years from earth and is the nearest star to us other than the sun. The typical distance between stars in a globular cluster is about one light-year, but at its core, the separation is comparable to the size of our solar system. Could you imagine having another star where Pluto is? If that were so, I would think we wouldn't have night anymore. That's precisely why I love to look at Globs because they're packed with ancient stars, and I love stars!

A typical Globular Cluster.

To see globular clusters up close and personal, I purchased a Meade LX200 ACF 12-inch scope. These are called GoTo telescopes in the strictest sense. The telescope is pre-programmed with the locations of millions of celestial objects and will point at them or GoTo them and have outstanding optics. A person can GoTo and see these objects with a push of a button.

I bought this telescope to take pictures of celestial objects and maybe take a picture of a UFO. At least, this was my thinking. The problem with trying to view something through a telescope and then trying to take a picture of that thing is a challenging endeavor. It is at least for me because you must set up the scope for one or the other. Plus, I would have had to buy a lot more equipment and purchase expensive computer software to do astrophotography, so I never set it up to take pictures. I guess it was all a pipe dream of sorts.

My Meade LX 200 ACF 12-inch telescope.

One evening, I looked through my telescope at the Orion Nebula, which is in the Orion Constellation. This constellation comes out all winter long, and I thought something strange about the number of stars there. You can see how many bright stars are supposed to be in the Orion Nebula in the image below. The brightest stars make up a trapezoid shape, which is named the Orion Trapezium. I have looked at the Orion Nebula for many years, and I knew exactly how many stars are supposed to be there.

The UFOs were in front of the Orion Trapezium. Notice that there are only 4 stars in the trapezium?

When I looked through my telescope, I witnessed more stars than usual. And there I sat, staring at them for a long time, maybe 4 or 5 minutes, wondering if I was seeing an aberration or something. Then one of the stars started moving, or one UFO began to move.

The three sightings coming up were one right after the other on consecutive nights like comrades in arms, as it were.

MINOR SIGHTING #1 Thursday 10/13/2011

On **Thursday 10/13/2011**, 5:30 a.m. until 5:45 a.m. I was looking at the Orion Nebula when one light started to move and I thought of following it. I knew I had just witnessed a UFO and was wondering where was it going. I viewed it for a couple of minutes, moving slowly from southeast to the northwest when two other lights started moving down my view from northwest to the southeast. They passed each other. When they did, about a minute later, the 1st UFO stopped. I went back to looking at the other moving star-like objects and following them. The other two moved for a couple of minutes more, and then they also stopped, which made them UFOs too. They were not very far from each other and only being about 1 ½ field of view apart. I stood there for another 10 minutes looking back and forth at those 3 UFOs, but they never moved again. I finally shut my scope down and went to bed.

MINOR SIGHTING #2 Friday 10/14/2011

Then on **Friday 10/14/2011**, I looked at the Orion Nebula when another light moved across my view. Again, I followed it. It proceeded in the same direction as the first UFO did on Thursday night, 10/13/2011, from southeast to northwest. It might have been the same UFO as the night before. I'm not sure because they're only points of light and have no other defining characteristics.

The UFO caught up with two more star-like objects. It slowed down to go at the same speed as the two it caught up with, and now all three were moving together. Nothing above our atmosphere can slow down so I knew I was most likely looking at UFOs. Those 3 UFOs caught up to 2 more UFOs that were stationary at the time, but then they started to move altogether—making a total of 5 UFOs now. Those 5 UFOs went in the same direction, southeast to northwest, and at the same speed. Then the 1st UFO slowed down, and then it stopped. It took a couple of minutes but then this UFO started moving again making a U-turn in the opposite direction, northwest to southeast. The UFO traveled in that direction until it finally stopped at the exact spot where I had 1st noticed it, back at the Orion Nebula. After that UFO stopped, I went back to see if I could pick up where the other 4 UFOs were, but they had either stopped and just looked like stars or were completely gone. I'm not sure what happened to them after that. I went back to the 1st UFO and stared intently at it for another 10 minutes or so. Nothing more happened this night, so I shut down my scope and went to bed.

MINOR SIGHTING #3 Saturday 10/15/2011

I woke during the night and had another strong urge to go outside to view the stars through my telescope. I was again looking through my telescope at the Orion Nebula, but this time it was at 2:15 a.m. on **Saturday, 10/15/2011**. Once more, there were more stars than there were supposed to be. It was just like the last two nights. When I'm expecting to see only four stars in the trapezium, and there are now seven in that location, I automatically know somethings amiss. I stared at those seven stars for a couple of minutes more. And I'm glad I did because three of the star-like objects or UFOs started to move in a westerly direction. They were moving very slowly for 10 minutes or so.

The three UFOs seemed the same size and color, all moving in the same direction and speed. It's as if they are moving like a squad of military jets or something. As I was watching them, all 3 UFOs slowed down, and then they all stopped. I kept staring at those three stationary UFOs for quite a while to see if anything else might happen, but nothing did. So, I turned off the scope and went to bed.

I could only see those UFOs through my Meade 12-inch telescope. I would take my eyes away from the scope but couldn't see them with my naked eye or binoculars. They know we can't see them with our naked eyes and need some better eye enhancer, and that's why I believe they hide in plain sight.

You know, while I am at it, I want to clarify something. Each of these star-like objects, although they are UFOs, does not mean that they are alien nor extraterrestrial ships. They could very well be ships developed by a government here on earth and not from a different planet. None of us knows exactly where these ships are made or who is flying in them. It could be an alien ship driven by a human or even vice versa.

The rest of 2011 passed by with no more sightings, but I was as diligent as I could be, looking at the night sky every night. No other sightings happened through most of 2012 either until the early winter of that year.

The UFO sighting below will be about one ship traveling in front of one of my favorite star clusters. It's called the Coathanger by us amateur astronomers because of a chance alignment of the stars in the cluster, making it look like an ordinary coathanger you would have in your closet. We call it the Coathanger, but its official name is Brocchi's Cluster, after American amateur astronomer D.F. Brocchi who created a map of it in the 1920s for calibrating photometers.

MINOR SIGHTING #4 Sarurday 11/17/2012

On **Saturday, November 17th, 2012**, I woke up again and grabbed my binoculars to go out to look up at the stars. I was looking at my favorite star cluster, Brocchi's Cluster. Another star-like object went right in front of it.

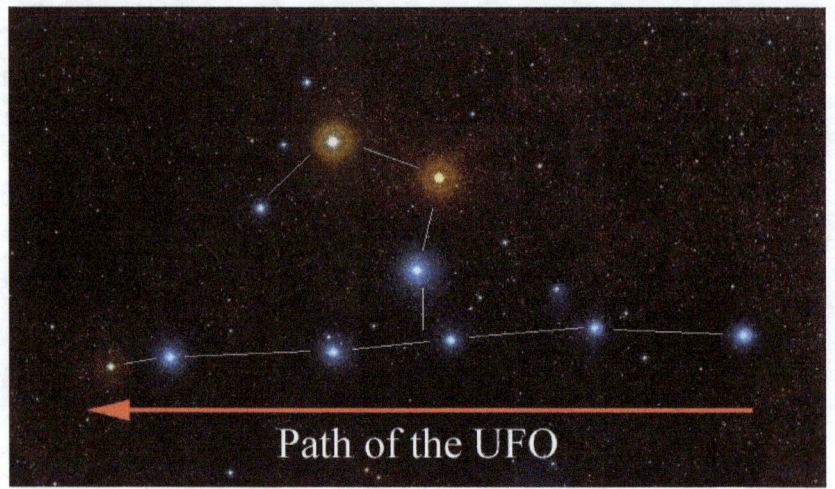

The Coat Hanger or Brocchi's Cluster.

I noticed what I thought to be a satellite going between the stars Arcturus and Vega. This craft was going so much slower than any satellite I have ever seen. It took over 10 minutes to go 40° degrees across the sky until it slowly vanished. There is just no way this sighting was anything close to a satellite because satellites don't move that slow. It takes a satellite, on average, a couple of minutes tops to go entirely across our skies. This object took ten minutes to cross the sky and 35 seconds just to pass in front of the six horizontal stars in the Brocchi's Cluster, which are very close to each other. It would take somewhere around 6 seconds for a satellite to traverse this cluster.

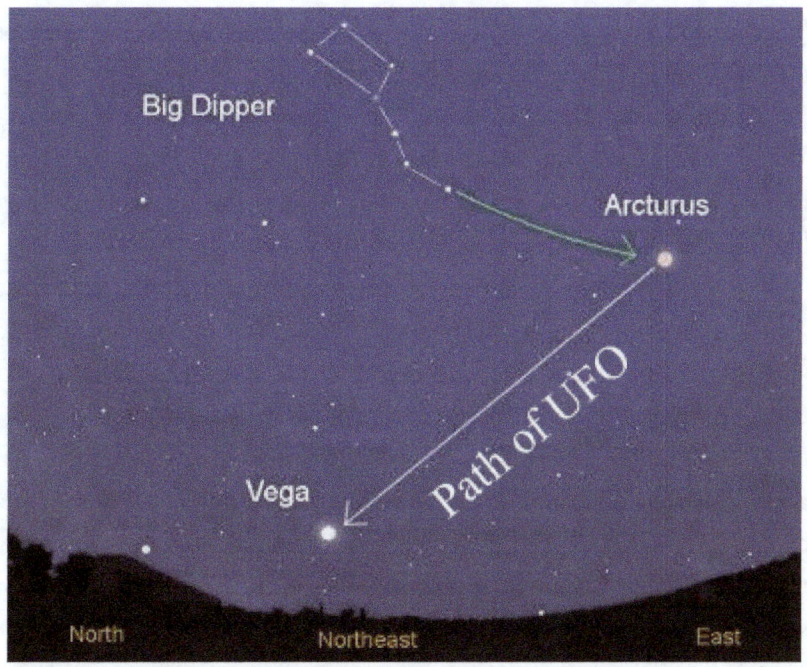

The Path of the UFO.

It can take the International Space Station (ISS) up to 4 – 5 minutes to completely cross the sky from horizon to horizon or 180° degrees, NOT 10 minutes to go 40° degrees. If we were to compare the ISS going this slow, it would mean that to traverse 180° degrees or from horizon to horizon would take 27 minutes! Which would be an impossible scenario. To slow the ISS down to this speed means the ISS would fall from the sky because it couldn't maintain enough angular momentum to keep circling the earth.

I have seen the ISS on seven different occasions and know what the International Space Station looks like when crossing the Phoenix skies. Once you see the ISS for the first time, you'll never forget what it looks like when it passes overhead. I know how bright it is and how long it takes for it to go across our skies. It's incredibly bright, and the dimensions are approximately 356 feet (109 meters) by 240 feet

(73 meters), or slightly larger than a football field and have a lot of reflective surface area. You really can't miss it.

That sighting above of a UFO between the stars Arcturus and Vega was on **November 17th, 2012,** close to 3 a.m. Then, for a couple of weeks in late 2013, I had two more sightings of multiple star-like UFOs.

Remember when I spoke of the bewitching hours and how UFOs come into and go away from our skies from 3:00 a.m. - 5:00 a.m.? There's a tremendous amount of star-like UFOs during that time, and this next sighting happened close to those times.

I thought these could be satellites but the thing that gave them away as UFOs was their color. Satellites are a bright white color because of the reflection of the sun off their metallic surfaces. If something above me is traveling across the sky and is blue or yellow or some other color, it's most likely a UFO rather than a man-made object. I did check the satellite location websites, and none of these were them, though.

MINOR SIGHTING #5 Sunday 09/29/2013

DESCRIPTION OF UFO EVENT: 4 UFOs zigzagged across the Phoenix skies on **Sunday, September 29th, 2013,** beginning at 5:00 a.m. and ending around 5:32 a.m.

At 4:45 a.m., I went outside of my house to the south side of the yard and gazed with my binoculars Bushnell 10 x 50 towards the zenith angle, and Polaris was visible.

1st incident: At 5:00 a.m., I noticed a small light-blue object traversing at an average satellite speed in a straight line. It crossed overhead on a trajectory from south to north and lost view when it went over my house.

2nd incident: At 5:06 a.m., I was still on the south side of the house. I saw another light, much brighter and a bluish-white color, more significant and much more vivid. This object was moving faster than the previous one. The trajectory was from north to south, and it was slightly overhead. I lost sight of it when it passed over the roof of the next-door neighbor's house on the south side.

3rd incident: At 5:26 a.m., I moved to the west side of the house, and by this time, I was facing south. Another much larger object appeared about four times more prominent, with a trajectory from southeast to northwest. It traversed slowly, much slower than any satellite I have ever seen, and it took a long time to cross overhead. It was angling across me overhead, and when it was on my right side or west, it seemed to disappear behind the Italian cypress tree, which is about 2 feet wide. I followed the UFOs trajectory but could not distinguish this light from the rest of the stars because I expected the UFO to pop up from behind the tree, but it didn't. I looked for the UFO, but I don't know whether it disappeared or merely stopped. Nothing in that location ever moved again. An analogy to explain the difference in sizes between the second sighting is that this star-like object would be the space station's brightness compared to a typical satellite. It was that bright.

4th incident: 6 minutes later, I walked around my house, facing south. At 5:32 a.m., I was gazing with my binoculars to the west. A much more significant, brighter yellowish light came into view from behind the same Cypress tree. But now, it had a trajectory from southwest to northeast, and it was moving very quickly. He lost sight of it within 30 seconds because it went over the horizon.

Just eight days later, on **Monday, October 7th, 2013**, I had yet another multiple star-like object sighting. What is incredibly weird about these two sightings is they never happened before these two events nor since. There were a lot of star-like UFOs zipping around to and fro. Usually, I'm up at these times and never witnessed anything like what was happening in the skies above Phoenix. I still wonder why there was so much activity in such a short period.

MINOR SIGHTING #6 Monday 10/07/2013

DESCRIPTION OF UFO EVENT: 8 UFOs zigzagged across the Phoenix skies on Monday, October 7th, 2013, beginning at 4:30 a.m. and ending around 5:30 a.m.

DESCRIPTION OF UFO EVENT: On 10/07/2013, I woke at approximately 4:25 to go outside to view the stars. Within minutes I saw star-like UFOs flying every which way. All the commotion started right at 4:30 a.m. I was lying on my lounge chair, facing south, looking around, and saw a bright blue light moving across the sky. It looked similar to a satellite, but I was not sure what it was. Then I saw another light and another and more. Below is a culmination of an hour of viewing the skies and the total amount of these -called satellites I observed.

Incident 1: At 4:47 a.m. I had been looking through my 10 x 50 Bushnell binoculars above me. I was facing south the entire time and saw an object looking like a satellite come into view. It moved from the northwest towards the southeast, passing over me, ending up on my left side. It stayed relatively straight from that point on, where I lost it about 45 degrees above the southeastern horizon.

Incident 2: At 4:50 a.m., again looking straight up, I noticed a bright object moving from the north towards the south. I lost the star-like object over the southern horizon.

Incident 3: At 4:52 a.m. I looked around for more objects when one came into view, moving from the north towards the south again, where I lost it just above the southern horizon.

Incident 4: At 5:05 a.m. Another bright object was moving from the north towards the south. It's as if all these were following each other from the north to the south. Again, I lost it just above the southern horizon.

Incident 5: At 5:12 a.m. I took note of another bright object that came into view, moving from the south towards the north, where I lost it just above the northern horizon this time.

Incident 6: At 5:18 a.m. I detected another bright object, moving from the south towards the north, where I lost it just above the northern horizon this time.

Incident 7: At 5:20 a.m. I observed yet another bright object, moving from the north towards the south this time, where I lost it just above the southern horizon again.

I'm not sure if any of these UFOs did a U-turn heading back north or not. I remember that the UFOs coming from the south and going north looked exactly like those heading in the opposite direction, moving from north to south.

Incident 8: At 5:30 a.m. I saw a bright object going from the west or my right towards the east, where I lost it above the eastern horizon.

Within 43 minutes, in the early morning hours of **Monday, October 7th, 2013**, eight objects flew every which way, crisscrossing the Phoenix skies. They all had the characterization of looking like satellites going across the heavens. Some were light blue, some yellow, some white. None seemed to be the same size either, some larger and some smaller.

The speed was inconsistent, with each moving at its own pace across the sky—some fast, some slow. None, though, were as ultra-fast as a meteor. Unfortunately, as far as I could tell, no object changed directions either. Whatever way they were pointing when I first observed them is the direction they kept going until I lost sight of them below the horizon. Several high-flying airplanes and a helicopter were flying at the same time too.

When a star-like UFO shows up, it's kind of fun, and I hold my breath a little because it could be a UFO. That is until I go to the satellite location websites and check to see if any of these are indeed satellites. Then either my balloon pops or I get very excited.

Below is another one of those exciting periods because none of these were satellites, but since I could not determine exactly what these were, they must go down in history as just another light going across the sky.

2013 went by without another UFO sighting. I kept looking but no more star-like UFOs until five years later, in 2018, when I witnessed something that was, without a doubt, a UFO. And I didn't need to check the satellite location sites online either.

MINOR SIGHTING #7 Wednesday 06/06/2018

On **Wednesday, June 6th, 2018**, the wife and I were outside, and I was looking again through my binoculars. This time I'm in a chair sitting up and facing south. I'm using my higher magnification 20 x 50 Bushnell binoculars, trying to see globular clusters up close and personal. Although these are twice as powerful as my 10 x 50's, they are challenging to track an object. If something came into view in the binoculars and put them down to see them only with my eyes, it's nearly impossible to relocate the object again. That's why I typically use the 10 x 50 binoculars because relocating an object is relatively easy.

As I'm looking around to the south side of my home, I see a globular cluster and get very excited. Above this globular cluster, I see a bright white star within the same field of view. It's stationary, so I don't think much about it and keep staring at the globular cluster while trying to keep the bright star within the same view. All of a sudden, the star-like object starts to move south toward the globular cluster.

Now, it has become a UFO. What else could that object be? I know of nothing else but a UFO. I see it going towards the southern horizon, and there it disappears. There were no blinking lights with this UFO, similar to the blinking lights on all our aircraft, so I knew it was not that. Just two weeks later after this last sighting, I came back from a trip and had another UFO sighting.

MINOR SIGHTING #8 Friday 06/22/2018

On **Friday, June 22nd, 2018**, just five days after getting back from Minnesota, I'm outside looking around. We went to Minnesota between June 7th and June 17th to see our two boys and two grandchildren. I didn't bring my binoculars with me so that I couldn't watch the skies up there.

I'm outside and take a guess what happens? It seems the bewitching hour starts all over because right at three o'clock in the morning, I start seeing star-like objects move. I notice what I believe to be a satellite and know that I need to have this point of light just out of my sightline while viewing it in the binoculars. More times than not, the UFOs fly in pairs or multiples of ships. Just like the sightings of multiple UFOs near the Orion Nebula above. The star came into view nearly overhead. I am watching this go across the sky, and as I do, I see the stars whizzing by and see a stationary star-like object or UFO start to move. Same speed, same direction, same brightness, and the same color. Same ship type, I am thinking! Buddies flying together, I guess. It's enjoyable being out between 3:00 a.m. and 5:00 a.m. here because the skies light up with UFOs doing whatever UFOs do.

MINOR SIGHTING #9 Saturday, June 23, 2018

The bewitching hour raised its fantastic head again, thank goodness. The next night, **Saturday, June 23rd, 2018**, I came out at 3:05 a.m. on that morning. When I wake and know I'm going outside to look through the binoculars, I always look at the clock to see what time it is just in case something tremendous happens, and I need to write it down.

The sightings of these star-like UFOs zipping to and fro is not enough, I think, to warrant me to document them. But if I see an actual ship where I can define its characteristics other than being star-like, well, then heck yeah, I'll get down as much as I can about the sighting to document it. If it's an actual ship, then maybe someone else has witnessed it, corroborating the evidence.

Anyway, I head outside, lay down on my patio chair again facing south, and what do you think happens? The minute I put the binoculars up to my eyes, I see a star-like object right overhead at my zenith and follow it, heading south. It's traveling kind of fast, but I can keep up with the fastest of them. Above I told you that I like to keep them almost out of view because they can meet up with others.

As this object traveled around 10 degrees, it slowed down a lot and nearly stopped, did a U-turn, and went back to where I first noticed it, but it kept going. As it did the U-turn, it became another UFO, of course. As I watched this UFO travel back to where I first witnessed it, another ship crossed its path, so I decided to follow it, but unfortunately, nothing else happened.

There were many objects that night flying to and fro, and I wished I had several people with me. I bet you that those UFOs would have stopped or gotten together or would have done something spectacular. It's hard when they buzz around like this because I am unsure which one I should keep an eye on.

To any extent, satellites cannot do U-turns. If they are moving, they are on a direct course flying mostly at or over 17,500 m.p.h. around our globe. They certainly never change their course as this one UFO did.

I have looked at the night skies of Phoenix for well over 25 years now. Every night I'm watching, seeking, and believing that UFOs are here. These UFOs are taking off from our airspace and going somewhere else, I'm sure of it. Well, as sure as I can be. I have come to understand that there is a pattern of what these UFOs are doing but I don't know why.

As you have read, these star-like objects are, in fact, UFOs because I have checked the satellite location software online against what I've witnessed above, and none were satellites.

If you want to have fun like I've been having fun all these years, I suggest that you look to the heavens too, and maybe one day you'll find yourself watching a bunch of UFOs like me. I love the bewitching hours because I can witness so much UFO activity.

MINOR SIGHTING #10 June 2019

I just had another sighting of a star-like UFO doing a U-turn in **June 2019**. It only did the U-turn once, and I lost it over the horizon. Since I've seen these star-like UFOs so often, it has almost become humdrum. When I see one doing some unusual maneuver, I don't get that excited about witnessing a star-like UFO anymore.

Well, that was the last sighting you will be reading about and I hope you enjoyed reading about my life with UFOs. You might be wondering if I should have had one of the many UFO investigation sites come out and talk with me about all the sightings I've had.

On most of my sightings, I did report them to the MUFON.com website and even had investigators come out to ask me questions about the sighting. MUFON is an acronym for the Mutual UFO Network, and I've heard talk that they do some fantastic UFO investigations, but I'm afraid I have to disagree with that assumption. They investigated each sighting I reported to them, but I chose not to include those reports in the book for several reasons.

The first and foremost was the investigator's conclusions about the sightings. They all seem to fall into one category; IFO or Information Only. So, what good would it have done for me to include their conclusion of "Information Only" on all my sightings into this book, I thought.

The second reason I didn't include their investigations was the other witnesses with me. I had other witnesses with me during the UFO sightings, but they never once questioned them about what they saw. Again, why include an incomplete analysis.

The third reason was the location of most of these sightings. I live no more than six miles from Sky Harbor International Airport. Not once did I read in any report the investigator mentioning that they contacted the airport to see if they saw anything on their RADAR screens. I would have thought the airport would be a great place to notice a UFO since they have a tremendous RADAR system. But no, they never once contacted them.

The fourth reason is I also live close to a U.S. Air Force base. Our house is 22 miles directly west of Luke AFB. If our airport weren't good enough to contact, surely this military installation would have been because they have an even better RADAR system than the airport. But no, they never contacted them either.

And the fifth and final reason was that although I had others with me during these different UFO sightings, they never once found other witnesses in Phoenix who might have seen what we saw. I just can't believe that I was the only person on earth to have witnessed these UFOs. And for all those reasons, I decided it would be better not to include those so-called investigative reports in this book.

These UFOs aren't all ours, nor could they all be alien. We need to accept that we are being visited by aliens and most likely have been given that technology for our own purposes. This is a real thing. Once everyone accepts and believes it, I think they will show themselves. Then the real party will start.

10

The Alien Agenda

"The Universe is a pretty big place.
If it's just us, seems like an awful waste of space."
Carl Sagan, from Contact the movie.

    The last chapter in this book will not be about any sighting I might have witnessed, so I apologize in advance. This chapter, to me at least, is still as exciting because I believe I know why the aliens are here. I wondered about all those sightings of so many different UFO ships. It got me thinking about why there are so many different kinds of craft with perhaps completely divergent aliens from varying planets. Following this logic then brings me to why are they here and what are they doing? I call this chapter The Alien Agenda because I will try and prove why the aliens of those UFOs are so interested in us humans.

    Throughout this book, I tried to answer some questions that had bothered me since I first witnessed the UFO in 1975 on Pipe Lake. I have already explained the gift that the universe at large could have given to me, but that only goes so far.

    Was it the universe, or was it a group of aliens that gave that gift to me, and if so, are there others like me that have this gift? I know of only one other like me and he has also had multiple sightings of UFOs. And he has also written a book about those sightings titled

UFOs First Person: A Lifetime of UFO Secrecy by Professor Dave Shoup. It is also sold at Amazon just like my book. Dave Shoup and I have become friends and I suggest you pick up his fascinating book.

Since I have witnessed so many different UFOs, many questions start coming across my mind like a train speeding downhill. Why the V shape UFO? For example, the delta wing or black triangular crafts have many varying characteristics like size, shape, solid in the middle, and open in the middle. These UFOs have changed quite a bit except for the color. They seem always to be black, as far as I can tell. The ship design is the only thing that changes.

We have known that triangular-shaped UFOs are one of the most common types observed. But why? I think the answer to that question is an alien race came here with that triangular or delta winged design and we copied it. But we needed help with that design shape, and they helped us with adding different angled surface areas to keep radar systems from see them on their screens. As far as them being colored black, I believe we humans chose that color to better camouflage our aircraft and they followed suit to keep everything coordinated. There's a great book; Triangular UFOs: An Estimate of the Situation by David Marler about this very subject. I think it's a must read, too.

In Chapter 8, I talked about the black triangular UFO I witnessed, and it was more of an isosceles shape. Are all these ships from one planet? And why the triangular shape? Before the military started seeing these triangular crafts, they tried their own type many years ago. It worked to a degree as a prop airplane, but when they moved the design into the jet stage, it became a way to create a high-speed jet capable of hiding from radar.

Here are a few designs of triangular or delta winged craft. Some are alien and some are man-made. Can you tell the difference?

When it comes to the alien plan, I can tell you what I believe in my heart but to actually prove it can be quite tricky. The UFOs and their extraterrestrial occupants will one day show up for all to see and we will, at that point, know for sure what has been going on. But for now, I will put forth my theories, and you can accept what I think is correct or completely deny it. Either way, it is up to you to take in all the information and decide what is the truth.

For me, I believe that there are and have been many different types of aliens visiting Earth over our entire history. Some alien species have a direct agenda that favors our development, while others have their own agenda and are not so pleasant. They are in constant competition for us and their own agenda. There are the spiritual service-to-others club and the non-spiritual service-to-self club, which I will speak more about a little later.

The only way to truly figure out what a space ferrying species of aliens would want with or for us is to compare what we would want, given the same situation. We will soon be space-traveling beings, and we will find and visit planets in different developmental stages. Some of those planets will have lower life forms on them like plants, while others will have plants and animals or what science calls flora and fauna.

Some of those planets that have fauna on them could have beings with much higher intelligence and self-awareness. On Earth, we humans are obviously self-aware. I think, therefore, I am. Basically, we are sentient beings. The word sentient comes from Latin, meaning feeling, and it describes things that are alive, able to feel and perceive, and show awareness or responsiveness. Having those senses makes something sentient or can smell, communicate, touch, see, or hear.

If you were to look in a mirror, you would know that it is your reflection you see. But say a dog was to look in that same mirror, she would think it is another dog trying to take over her territory. She would not know it was her in that mirror. A dog is a sentient being but doesn't have higher brain functions like self-awareness.

Let me back up a few hundred million years to the start of it all. I am quite sure that there have been extraterrestrials flying all over the universe and for billions of years. I think they find planets capable of harboring life and going to that planet to check them out. If there's intelligent life like here on Earth, then one of the two camps I spoke of earlier jockey for position for that intelligent life.

What would we do if we were to visit another planet outside of our solar system? We already know there is exo-planets outside of the solar system. In just a few decades from now, we will be able to photograph those distant worlds and know their atmosphere's chemical makeup. We will be able to know beyond a shadow of a doubt that some alien planet could harbor life.

Take a star system that is relatively close to us. For example, Proxima Centauri is only 4.3 light-years away. We have plans today to send a fleet of micro labs to that system via lasers, which will drive those little labs all the way there. We will have a close-up view of that planet because these micro labs will contain cameras and other scientific instruments. As our science evolves, we will send other robotic labs that will go there and actually sniff the atmosphere, photograph the surface, and hopefully see other humanoid type beings.

If they exist, we will see what stage of development they are in and if they are like us. Just for the sake of argument, we could find this species to be in an industrial stage of development. Just like we were 150 years ago. We can make an educated guess that they will go from this point in a few short decades or a couple of centuries to being a space ferrying species, so we'll want to go ourselves and meet them. That's when we develop the wormhole, that is. And who knows, maybe when they read my wormhole chapter, they will understand that it doesn't take an enormous amount of energy to open up a wormhole to travel to the stars.

Let me propose a few what-if scenarios for that meeting; Of course, when our first astronauts go to the planets with intelligent life, their missions will be pure science. They will want to study the planet's flora and fauna plus the inhabitants of those planets. Later on, not only scientists can go to other worlds, but anyone from any country will be able to cross the universe and do whatever they see fit when they land. And that's the million-dollar question right there; will we land? As a species, will we interfere with another world by landing?

When our science evolves to the point that anyone with enough money could have their own spaceships, to me at least, all hell is going to break loose. That's because anyone with an agenda can go to any planet. Unless we, as an earthly species, are on the same page, as it were. We all will have to have some regulatory policy in place not to screw up another planet like we screwed up this one.

In the fictional television show Star Trek the prime directive, which was also known as the "non-interference directive" is a guiding principle of Starfleet, prohibiting its members from interfering with the internal and natural development of alien civilizations. The prime directive applies particularly to civilizations that are below a certain threshold of technological, scientific, and cultural development; preventing starship crews from using their superior technology to impose their own values or ideals on them. We need a policy like this one or things will be as bad as they were when men started sailing the oceans.

Vikings sailed to North America around 1000 years ago. But we know very little about that voyage and even less about any meeting with the new people of that land. We know that when Europeans moved to North America, it didn't end well for the native peoples. When Christopher Columbus sailed across the Atlantic in 1492 and landed in the Bahamas, we have done nothing but overtake every civilization that was in our way.

Some went to convert those people to their religion. The Europeans thought that that would be best for them since they were looked upon as savages and had no spirituality.

They thought so little for others, like Africans, that they enslaved them starting in 1619 in America. The first 19 or so Africans to reach the colonies England struggled to establish arrived in Point Comfort, Virginia, near Jamestown, in 1619, brought by British privateers who had seized them from a captured Portuguese slave ship.

In every instance, the Europeans absolutely destroyed the place they landed at, killing millions of those people by the diseases the Europeans carried. Or by actually murdering those that would not convert to their religion or give up their riches. Slaves were usually baptized in Africa before embarking because they were seen as being unholy.

Some of those people's plan was to go looking for gold. They stole billions of dollars' worth of their precious metals like gold and silver. They were bringing back those riches for the kings from the countries they served.

They also inadvertently left invasive species like dogs, cats, rats, hogs, chickens, horses, and other non-native animals that decimated the wildlife. Do you know that the common House Sparrow bird is actually from the Middle East? The sparrow was introduced into Brooklyn, New York, America, in 1851, and that's why America is inundated with that bird.

Some islands had been so isolated that most of the animals on those islands had no fear of predators, wiping those animals out. We have an extinction scenario going on right now. The Yunnan lake newt went extinct in China in 1979 due to exotic fish and frogs in their habitats. The Hawaiian thrush went extinct by 1985 due to invasive predators, and the Guam broadbill went extinct when they introduced the Brown Tree snake to its habitat in 1983. This same scenario goes on like that on every continent around the globe. So, if we don't want history to repeat itself, we better have something in place that all of us can agree on before someone goes to another planet.

What if, instead of scientists going, the people on those spaceships were of a particular religious denomination? What if those people were all Muslim, Jewish or Buddhist, or even extremist Christians? Once they landed and found higher intelligent, sentient beings, would they not want them converted? Would they require them to be baptized to save the souls?

Christians believe that this is an act of obedience symbolizing the believer's faith in a crucified, buried, and risen Savior, Jesus Christ.

What if those humanoid type beings on those other planets could not get the true reason? What would those space-traveling extremists do then?

The mere fact that a ship from space shows up on their planet could make them believe the occupants are Gods. Arthur C Clarke was a brilliant futurist and writer. Still, he is probably most widely known for the third of his famous three laws, "Any sufficiently advanced technology is indistinguishable from magic." Knowing this, these space ferrying people, or what I would call religious fanatics, could even pretend they are a God and that they will save their souls. The beings on this planet would be freaking out and dropping to the ground, fearing these beings from space and scared for their own lives. They might even start a religion based on what they just were witnessed. Does any of this sound familiar?

In the 18th century, it was a widely held belief that white Europeans in the United States were destined to expand across North America. This was called Manifest Destiny. They wouldn't let anyone get in their way and stop them from achieving that goal, no matter how many native savages they have to convert or kill! Remember when I was talking about being a service-to-self species? Well, there you go, the white Europeans were a service-to-self people.

Now let's look at a more optimistic scenario. What if the people on those ships thought life is so precious that to hurt a fly would go against their belief system? What if they knew that raising any being to a higher level of spirituality and vibration bordering on enlightenment would start them on a beautiful journey of service-to-others rather than service-to-self? If they can bring a being to this level, then all the beings on those planets would live in total bliss and harmony and would never conceive of conflicts with others.

There would be no need for any military. There would be no need for weapons of any type, be it sport, self-protection, or the atomic bomb. There would be no need for borders or creating separate countries because there would be no need to achieve power. Creating borders gives someone power. You could write an entire book about power and borders, but I digress.

If there weren't any of the things above, the world would be a better place. We would be one with a higher power, the Infinite Creator, and there would be no reason for religions either! And those people who serve others would also know that those beings they met on the planets they visit would do everything they could for others too and find that this way of life is really the only way to live. Doing things for other people is a blessing for me, and I wouldn't have it any other way.

If that planet has a monetary system similar to what we have on our planet, there would be no need to spend it trying to defend themselves or to kill others. And the monies could then be put to good use. Again, this could be a whole other book to explain.

Knowing that we could interfere with other planets' development, has there been any interference with this planet? I believe there have been long term experiments done by different groups of aliens on our planet, and thus the title The Alien Agenda. I think they developed the ape species that could walk upright and experiment on those apes to help them evolve. Then evolution took over, allowing a change into the species we now know as Homo-sapiens.

There have been several hominoid species living simultaneously on this planet, starting around 1,800,000 years ago to the present.

- Homo-erectus (1,800,000 - 140,000 years ago)
- Homo-heidelbergensis (700,000 – 200,000 years ago)
- Homo-denisova (600,000 – 200,000 years ago)
- Homo-neanderthal (200,000 to 30,000 years ago)

- Home-floresiensis (100,000 – 60,000 years ago)
- Homo-sapiens (300,000 to present)

At least six different Homo species living on Earth together around 200,000 years ago, and Homo-sapiens outlasted them all. We must have had the right tweak in our DNA genome to survive this long. Until we find the master plan in our DNA, scientists will still believe that evolution carried the weight.

We already know how to mix the DNA of different species for our benefit. All dogs came from wolves. The chickens we eat are not the chickens from a thousand years ago. They grow faster and are much larger. The wheat we eat has slowly changed from grasses eons ago.

All of our crops have some DNA changes done to them. Recombinant DNA technology or genetic engineering has made it possible to genetically engineer organisms currently on the market, including plants resistant to certain insects, plants that can tolerate herbicides, and crops with modified oil content. If we can do this with the little bit of knowledge we now have, just think what an alien species, which could be billions of years more advanced, would be able to do.

I, on the other hand, believe in Intelligent Design. Intelligent Design is a religious argument for God's existence or what I call the Infinite Creator, presented by its proponents as an evidence-based scientific theory about life's origins. Like me, advocates of evolution claim that certain universal features and living things are explained better by an intelligent cause, not an undirected process such as natural selection or evolution.

Two scientists in Kazakhstan who worked for over 13 years on the Human Genome Project believe in an intelligent design to our DNA and that it had to come from an extraterrestrial source. I believe in this same logic. Change the word God with Alien, and you can better understand why I think aliens had a hand in our development. And why we as Homo-sapiens so-called evolved compare to any other Homo species.

For now, let's skip forward. How was humankind developed over those eons creating the race of Homo-sapiens we see today? As I stated above, many human-type beings were sharing the planet simultaneously, but Homo-sapiens were the only species to survive today. Why is that? If Homo-sapiens have evolved into an intelligent design or master plan, could it be that this is the reason we see so many UFOs today? And did our ancestors see as many ships as we see?

Homo-sapiens were the mammal of choice since we had the largest brain and could learn best and fastest. It was social innovations and better tool-making that is believed to have helped us survive. Were we taught how to make better tools? I think that the aliens engineered this larger brain through tweaks in our DNA and all the others fell by the wayside, as it were.

Earth is a water world and harbors an enormous amount of life. The aliens knew Earth was here and had plenty of oxygen and water eons ago when there was only microbial life. Because the Earth had wild climate changes creating snowball Earths, they had to bring in the moon to stop this from occurring so that multi-cellular life could take a foothold on land. Scientists believe that we came from the oceans, and animals evolved into reptiles and mammals.

It worked too well because the reptiles or what we know as dinosaurs ruled the Earth for 135 million years yet could not evolve past a walnut-sized brain and into an intelligent species. The dinosaurs had to be eliminated, so the aliens brought in a large enough asteroid and slammed it into Earth, thus killing off the dinosaurs but NOT mammals.

Once mammals evolved to an ape-like species, the DNA tweaking started. That also worked too well since there were six Homo species at the same time on Earth around 200,000 years ago. That is when they tweaked Homo-sapiens DNA, creating a much smarter species, and thus here we are, writing a book telling you about our intelligent design, and you reading this and understanding it.

This might come as a shock to you, but some aliens walk the Earth today. Some so closely resemble our design that if one stood next to you, there would be no way you would know they were extraterrestrial. Our body and mind plan are something that has worked many times on many distant worlds.

Also, we are not the only species in the universe that has developed the atomic bomb either. There had been wars on those distant planets that have used that same technology. The aliens do not want us to spread war or use atomic hostilities once we become a space ferrying species. We have to change our ways and do it quickly. I read somewhere on the internet that when we set off a nuclear explosion, this screws with the universe's spirituality somehow. Until we get to the point where we can measure spirituality, I'll have to take their word for it.

Canada's ex-defense minister, Paul Hellyer, claims aliens will give us more technologies if we'd stop wars. Mr. Hellyer, who has long insisted that aliens have visited Earth for many years, says that when aliens saw the atomic bomb, they decided that we were a significant threat to the cosmos. That's because the universe is teeming with advanced beings with a high degree of spirituality and enlightenment.

As I stated earlier, we could be a service-to-others species or service-to-self, and service-to-self just doesn't cut it out there in the greater universe. They do not want us to be a society fighting each other and possibly destroying ourselves or the Earth. The aliens understand all too well that we are now a space ferrying race and could bring the atomic technology with us. They want us to be a more enlightened species. If we are to go to other stars, they don't want a society that takes over other beings. They want one that will bring others into this enlightened state because ALL life is precious.

This is why I believe they helped create Homo-sapiens and create our religions, but we have not done so well with this either. I say they helped with the world's religions because this was one of the only ways that would work to stop us from killing each other. It's a sin to kill someone in Christianity, and we would go to Hell if we committed such a heinous act.

We have a dichotomy of 2 worlds. One of a peace-loving people and one with wars, and that just won't cut it if we travel to the stars. Even in our world's political systems, we have two large governing bodies: a Democracy or Socialism system or service-to-others. And a Communism, Totalitarianism, Dictatorial or service-to-self society. A common dichotomy of human ethics is good versus evil, which is usually perceived as the dualistic antagonism of the opposites. This can be taken as good will always defeat evil.

What about all the different inhabitants of those UFOs? Are there positive or negative groups of aliens and agendas that are associated with the UFOs? Positive alien groups as in service-to-others? The answer is yes. There are both camps of aliens out there and here on Earth. One being highly spiritually enlightened and another that clearly has done experiments on humans. And it is not to save us. It is to save themselves, which I will elaborate shortly.

How did the modern story of UFOs start anyway? The modern story is very fascinating. I believe this is how the story goes; around 1952, astronomers discovered several large objects in space moving toward the Earth. At first, they thought that they were asteroids. Later evidence proved that the objects could only be spaceships since they were slowing down.

When the objects reached the Earth, they took up a very high orbit around the equator. There were several huge ships, and their actual intent was unknown. In 1952, a joint operation by the NSA (National Security Agency) and the CIA (Central Intelligence Agency) was launched – Project Sigma.

The purpose of the operation, which was carried out under President Eisenhower's immediate supervision, was to establish a productive partnership between human beings and the aliens on those ships. Project Sigma and a new project, Plato, through radio communications using the binary computer language, 0's & 1's, the primary computer code used today, was able to arrange a landing that resulted in face-to-face contact with the alien beings from another planet.

There are a number of alleged meetings with an extraterrestrial group and President Eisenhower at Edwards Air force base on February 20-21, 1954 that corresponded to a formal First Contact event. The excuse to get the president out of Washington was that Eisenhower was going on a golfing vacation in Palm Springs, California. On the appointed day, the President was spirited away to the air force base, and the excuse was given to the press that he was visiting a dentist.

Eisenhower met with a group of human-looking aliens with blonde hair, and blue eyes called the Nordics because they look like they are from Scandinavia. This alien group offered to help us with our spiritual development. They demanded that we dismantle and destroy all of the world's nuclear weapons as the primary condition. They refused to exchange technology, citing that we were spiritually unable to handle the technology we possessed. They believed that we would use any new technology to destroy each other. This race claimed that we were on a path of self-destruction, and we must stop killing each other, stop polluting the Earth, stop raping the Earth's natural resources, and learn to live in harmony.

These terms were met with extreme suspicion, especially the primary condition of nuclear disarmament. It was believed that meeting those conditions would leave us helpless in the face of an obvious alien threat. We also had nothing in history to help with the decision. Nuclear disarmament was not considered within the United States' best interest, and the overtures were rejected. These were the Etherians or Nordics, and they are a highly spiritual race and were just trying to look out for the human race's welfare.

Depiction of the Nordics – Etherians from the Pleiades star cluster

Later in 1954, a race of large nosed Grey aliens met Eisenhower at Holloman Air Force Base in New Mexico. This led to his second meeting with aliens. There was three round craft; one landing close to Air Force One, one hovering above, and one subsequently disappearing from view. The historical event had been planned in advance, and details of the treaty had been agreed upon. Eisenhower boarded the craft, and when he reappeared, he had signed the Treaty of Greada with the occupants, Grey Aliens.

He and the aliens had negotiated the following:

- We would not be involved in their affairs, and they would not become involved in ours.
- They would help us with developing new technology
- They would not make a treaty with any other nation on Earth
- They could abduct humans for various experiments but had to provide names of all those they abducted to Earth's Majestic 12 committee
- The public would not be informed about the existence of extraterrestrial

The problem with this scenario, to me at least, is the Etherians. A species so highly evolved as to come here in the first place and contact just one person on Earth. They surely would have known of the other country states in the world since this was just after World War II. Most of Europe was rebuilding everything back as it was. There were news reports worldwide talking about Germany, the USSR, France, England, Japan, and others involved in the war. To me, the prime directive should have been in place, and even if they thought that they needed to talk to someone, why on God's green Earth only talk with Eisenhower?

The problem with this situation was who they were talking to, President Eisenhower. If you don't remember, before being president, Eisenhower was General Eisenhower. He was the Supreme Allied Commander of the Allied Expeditionary Force. Serving in a dual role until the end of hostilities in Europe in May 1945. In these positions, he was charged with planning and carrying out the Allied assault on Normandy's coast in June 1944 and the liberation of western Europe and Germany's invasion. It was he who helped defeat Germany in World War II. He was not as much a politician as a war General.

I would have thought that they would make contact but not release any more information until all the world leaders were there to hear what they had to say. To give Eisenhower the full power to talk for the entire world was ludicrous and an insane proposition, to say the least, and it indeed backfired! It has been backfiring ever since.

A secret treaty was then formed with the long-nosed Gray aliens where the aliens would not interfere in our affairs, and we would not interfere with theirs. We would let them do what they want and also establish underground bases here in exchange for alien technology.

The treaty between Eisenhower and the grey aliens was created for both parties involved. Each wanted something the other had. We want technology. Technology as in spaceships that can go to the stars. Knowledge on how to get a wormhole open and then get to those stars. Cloaking technologies to hide our ships or jets so that other countries cannot see us coming. Very powerful weapon technology and many other things. Anything in science fiction now has become science fact! Want a group of our people to visit Mars? No problem, we have been on Mars for decades. Live on the Moon? Been there, done that too.

The eventual treaty with the Greys not only gave permission to increase the amount of UFO sightings so the general public will become better aware that they are here it also, and get this, it gave the Grey aliens permission to abduct a certain amount of humans and do experiments on as many as was obligated in the treaty. They told us they needed to do experiments on humans because their sun was a red giant star and their planet was almost inhospitable for life and that they were on the brink of extinction and needed to meld with humans so they could survive. The treaty stated that they would abduct only a few humans and give a list of names to the government of who they abducted. They were allowed to do general tests on cows and humans but do no harm to the human abductee. They would erase the abductee's memory so no emotional harm would be done too.

Now comes the Doh! moment and what has been backfiring all these years. After the Betty and Barney Hill abduction, the government realized that the Grey extraterrestrials had broken the treaty! They were not telling the government about all the people they were abducting. Betty and Barney Hill were not on the list of abductees. There was no oversight on our part. The government has had little to no power to enforce it because their hands are tied. You try working with a being that can cloak right in front of your eyes; can hide from all of our technologies; can wipe out the memory of the beings they are studying (humans) at least partially, and that can switch conscientiousness/souls between people, and yes, you read that correctly.

Think of it in this way, if you were to make a treaty with an ant society, would you really adhere to such a treaty or just blow it off? Most of us would just blow it off because we feel so superior to an ant that we do not even really care if we step on them and kill them, do we?

I think this is the issue with making a treaty with beings so far in advance of us that some of them feel like we are all just ants, especially the Reptilian race of extraterrestrials. You read that correctly. There is a race of beings that cater to the Grey's called the Reptilians! They look like huge dinosaurs, and they do not like humans.

A LIFE WITH UFOS

The Grey's – Reptilians are basically doing what they want when they want—experimenting on humans at will. They have been creating a Grey – Human hybrid. Extraterrestrials known as Alien-Human Hybrids are created through processes and procedures that occur during and after the abduction of, or visits with, humans by aliens with advanced intelligence.

The stages include:

1. Capture
2. Examination
3. Conference
4. Tour [of the ship]
5. Otherworldly Journey
6. Theophany [the appearance of a deity]
7. Return
8. Aftermath.

This is a depiction of the Reptilians. I would not want to meet this thing in a dark alley.

Their activities and possible motives for their interaction with humans were not because they as a race are dying but something much more sinister. The beings are planning to supplant humans on Earth in favor of their new human hybrid race. Or the hybrid race will be introduced to change the DNA of humans on Earth slowly, and the process will gradually occur so as not to draw attention. Or provide any provable evidence within the standard lifetime of humans. Or the human hybrid race will be introduced to change the DNA of humans on Earth rapidly, and the process will occur in the "blink of an eye" at the time of the Beings' choosing. Or when a catastrophic event occurs to our planet. Due to their ability to manage time events and time travel, they would determine when and how this catastrophic event will happen and how humanity's endgame will unfold.

In chapter 9, when I witnessed that huge black triangular craft, I wondered why were they in my neighborhood? I also thought to myself, why was I up at that particular time?

I have woken up with strange cut marks and scratches on my legs. I used to snore, so I went to sleep and got a CPAP machine and mask. That stands for Continuous Positive Airway Pressure, so when you start to snore, it is because your throat closes down. Positive air pressure blows through the mask you are wearing and forces your throat open with positive airflow allowing you to breathe again. What is so strange is that I had some scratches on my legs on one of the nights, and the chin strap for the CPAP mask was off. You literally have to unbuckle one part of the mask to get that strap off. The strap had never ever done that before nor since. It takes me or someone else to unbuckle the mask to release the chin strap. There is just no way for me to do this in my sleep either. Doesn't that sound a little scary?

And check this out. All these years of wearing the mask during the night, I never check how long it was on after I wake in the morning. I had an ah-ha moment and thought to check the time. I slept for what I thought was eight and a half hours but my time on the machine only showed six hours of wearing the mask! Now I was really freaked out. Where did the other hour and a half go?

My lovely wife had a triangular mark on her wrist that lasted there a long time and then went away. It disappeared only after we contemplated getting it tested for any unusual substances. She could not feel like there was an object under the skin, just the mark. How can a person wake up one morning and have a triangular mark on your wrist, and the next morning the mark was gone?

I once read about a guy that saw a UFO while he was driving, and the next thing he remembers, he was 10 miles from where he first saw the ship. It was 30 minutes later, and his shirt was on backward, so his buttons were on his back, and he does not remember a thing! Now that is freaky.

Whatever the reason, we will not have the same Earth in a few years as we have now. I am not trying to scare you with this information. It's just a different scenario that might or might not happen.

There is a higher government than the elected officials we have now, and they control all aspects of aliens and spaceflight. The NASA we know of today is a cover for what is really happening in space. The higher government, and the aliens that have been here for time immemorial, are definitely doing things that NONE of us really knows what.

Time will tell, and I think that time will be somewhere around 2047 at the latest. It could be anytime from now until then. I believe the scenario will be something like 100 years after the crash of an alien ship in 1947 in Roswell, New Mexico, which will be an acceptable amount of time for humans to get used to seeing and dealing with UFOs and the extraterrestrial question.

Many people have seen UFOs even before the 1947 Roswell incident. Just ask a pilot from either side of World War II. They had alien ships following them called foo fighters, which were glowing orbs and seen on both sides of the conflict. And remember the orb UFOs flying around the people of Basil, Switzerland? I will wager that there has been UFOs seen for many century's

Where have the aliens been hiding all this time? This next part might be the strangest part of this entire chapter. They have been hiding in plain sight, and I don't mean up in the night sky.

I will give you a few examples of where I believe they are. The higher government has been creating underground bases here on Earth and using them with the Grey's.

Here are a few examples of where they're suspected to be hiding:

- Dulce, New Mexico
- They are at area 51 in Nevada
- They have a base on the backside of the moon
- They are in Lake Baikal in Russia. Russian divers had an accidental meeting under the water that caused a few divers' deaths
- They were seen coming out of a farmer's swamp in Australia
- They are under nearly all the world's oceans
- They are in almost every large lake in the world
- Most likely in every state in the union and everywhere else on Earth
- They and we are in an extensive cave system on Mars
- They and we are on some of Jupiter's moon Ganymede

There is an organization, The Galactic Federation of Planets, that many different alien species and our higher government are members. Who is where, and what are they doing? They are everywhere, and as far as I can tell, there is a tremendous number of different aliens in and around our solar system and walking around the Earth.

What if our development was advanced by just ten thousand years or a million years, which is a blink of an eye in a cosmological sense? If you did not realize it, our solar system is only about 4.5 billion years old while the universe is 13.7 billion years old. That is over 9 billion years longer on an evolutionary track, and there are many different aliens out there that are that highly evolved.

The theory or conjecture above is what I believe happened throughout our history is what I think is going to happen. We do not know what had been going on, nor do we know what is about to occur. I have gathered information from different sources to develop my theory, and I could be completely mistaken, of course. Until they show up on the white house lawn, none of us will know this truth. We cannot wait for our government to come forward. They have made this perfectly clear. It is up to all of us to demand the aliens show themselves. In the first words of our constitution, it states, We The People. We, the people, have required a change in the past. If enough of you come forward and demand they tell us what we want to know, we can achieve change.

To end this chapter with a bang, I have collected what I believe to be all the alien races known so far from A-Z:

Alpha Draconians - Origin – Terra
Amphibians - Origin – Unknown
Andromedins - Origin – Andromeda
Arcturians - Origin – Bootes

Atlans - Origin – Living in caverns below Earth
Cetians (Tau Cetians) - Origin – Cetus
Dwarfs - Origin - Unknown
Eva-Borgs - Origin - Cyborg servants for the Grey alien race
Grey's (short) - Origin – Zeta Reticuli
Grey's (tall) - Origin - Orion
Grey/Human Hybrid - Origin - Human and Grey mixing
Iguanoids - Origin - Orion
Janosian - Origin - Janos
Korendians - Origin - Korendor / Bootes
Lyrans - Origin - Lyra
Mantas (insectoids) - Origin - possibly the Draco system
MIB - Origin – Bio-Synthetic race made by Draconians
Moon-Eyes -Origin - Race that lived in the caverns below Earth
Mothmen - Origin - Unknown
Nagas - Origin - Ancient Earth
Nordics - Origin - possibly the Pleiades star cluster
Pleiadeans - Origin - Pleiades
Procyonians - Origin - Procyon / Canis Minor
Reptilians - Origin - Alpha Draconi
Sirians - Origin - Sirius star system
Teros - Origin - Planet Jomon, Constellation Arcturus
Ummites - Origin - Ummo, Virgo

I sincerely hope you enjoyed the book as much as I did writing about my life with UFOs. This all might sound crazy, but all I can say is I have honestly witnessed 74 ships of at least eight different designs so far. I say so far because I still see UFOs.

I wanted to talk about one more item. We keep saying to each other that the government needs to come clean and admit they know about these UFOs. We need to admit this to ourselves first. The point is this, in the 60's we stood up to the government and said stop the Vietnam War, give the disabled and all women equal rights under the law. One of my heroes, Martin Luther King, and others did the same for the black communities. And as of this writing, we're marching in nearly every city in the world because Black Lives Matter! No lives matter until ALL lives matter!!!

The point is WE, THE PEOPLE, as in our constitution's first words, need to march on Washington D.C. and demand change. Please help others to change too. We need to get the UFO question answered and help stop others from thinking this subject is equal to something to laugh at or that we're crazy and hallucinating. I believe the case for UFOs can become a serious subject worth scientific investigation. Trust me, they are here and have been since time immemorial!

Namaste and God bless.

ABOUT THE AUTHOR

After leaving the U.S. Air Force and moving back in with my parents, I met Roxanne Cleveland. After a few years of being with Roxy, I worked at various jobs until I interviewed for and accepted a managerial position. This was in 1976, and the same year I married my 1st wife, Roxanne. We had two boys, Tony, born in 1978, and Steve, born 5 1/2 years later in 1983.

Tony has grown to be a wonderful and caring man and a better father than I ever was and a great son with two children of his own, Blake, 21, and Kenna is 18. I absolutely adore my grandchildren.

Steven has grown to be a loving and understanding man as well and is a man anyone could look up to, and I am so very proud of him and Tony.

Roxanne and I divorced in 1988 and have remained friends.

Although I loved being the manager of The Energy Shed, I decided it would be more profitable if I became an HVAC salesperson. I accepted a position at Sedgwick Heating and Air Conditioning and sold to general contractors building new homes and heating and air conditioning to the general public.

I was also a salesman for another HVAC company, Vogt Heating and Air in Minneapolis. I was in HVAC sales for 13 years until I had triple bypass heart surgery, which, thankfully, ended that career.

Near the end of selling HVAC, I created SubContractorsCreditReportingService.com in 1993, which was an internet site devoted

ABOUT THE AUTHOR

to finding negative information about the general contractors/home builders that I and others had to work with, which was not fun. Arguably, the first and only company in the world that could offer information about general contractors/home builders on the Internet. I decided to change that cumbersome name and created ContractorFacts.com.

ContractorFacts.com was an online service that allowed subcontractors and all consumers to search millions of records from multiple data sources regarding individual contractors and companies, delivering an instant snapshot of financial liabilities that help them make wise hiring and business decisions.

Some of the sites that check on contractors today use the information that the contractor supplies. Or the info is provided by the person the contractor worked with, which could distort the results. That's how Yelp gets their data, but nowhere near as accurate as getting the information from the court systems and other non-biased sources.

Knowing a great business model, I looked for a way to stop selling HVAC to general contractors and retrain in a different job that would help me with ContractorFacts.com.

I found a school in Tempe, AZ, that would retrain me, the University of Advancing Computer Technologies. At age 39, I decided it was time to go to college to improve my presence on the Internet.

On April 28th, 1996, we moved to Phoenix, Arizona. A couple of weeks later, I signed up for school. I graduated from the University of Computer Technologies, now its new name being on the dean's list every semester, and graduated top of my class. I earned an Associate of Arts degree in Multimedia.

I was retrained as a Webmaster and was sought after by elite companies such as Nabisco and Motorola. My position was to control all aspects of their worldwide online content. As a Webmaster, I created

ABOUT THE AUTHOR

many different types of websites. I was a Webmaster for the last 12 years of my working career. From 1996 until 2008, when I became disabled, I created over 700 websites.

While in school and after graduation, I kept offering subscriptions to ContractorFacts.com. In a press release in 2005 at PRWeb.com for The American Subcontractors Association of Arizona, in which I was a member, I was nominated for the prestigious "Innovator of the Year Award" for my role in developing ContractorFacts.com. I sold off the assets to ContractorFacts.com to a company in Minnesota and no longer have anything to do with the company.

I am now married to my third and last wife and best friend, Sharon. She and I are two peas in the same pod. We like all the same things and act the same way, crazy at times. And I absolutely enjoy life with her, even though we are both disabled and don't work anymore. We live in Phoenix, Arizona, of course, in a beautiful 3-bedroom home near the city of Tempe border and enjoying life to the fullest.

ACKNOWLEDGMENTS

I want to thank my immediate family, Sharon, my wife, and my two sons, Tony and especially Steve. Steve has been one of my rocks that inspired me to write this book. Since that fateful day on the Mississippi when he and I were fishing, and the two large round and dull silver UFOs were parked above us, he has watched the skies and has given me much help with this book. Thank you, Steve and Tony. I love you guys and appreciate you so very much.

Sharon has been with me on this project, helping me in so many ways, too. I would write things and bounce them off on her. She has been so very helpful to me. Plus, we were able to see 27 UFO orbs together, which made that sighting so enjoyable. Without her, I don't think I could have finished this book. Thank you, sweetheart. You are my best friend and the love of my life!

And if it weren't for my 5th-grade teacher who inspired me and gave me a chance to see the skies through a telescope, I would not have been looking up and seeing so many of God's splendor and all the different UFOs.

I would also like to thank my ex-wife Roxanne Groschen, my ex-brother-in-law, and little brother Brian Cleveland. You guys helped me beyond words with the Pipe Lake incident.

Thank you, Kelsey, and your three children for being with me during the fireball UFO and the acrobatics it performed. I hope it wasn't too scary for your children.

ACKNOWLEDGMENTS

And the stranger, Bill, who was with me in front of the 7-Eleven for being with me while witnessing the bell-shaped UFO.

I did get input from some of them, so it helped me tell their story and how they felt when those UFOs showed up.